Sexual Correctness

Sexual Correctness

The Gender-Feminist Attack on Women

by WENDY MCELROY

McFarland & Company, Inc., Publishers
Jefferson, North Carolina, and London

British Library Cataloguing-in-Publication data are available

Library of Congress Cataloguing-in-Publication Data

McElroy, Wendy
    Sexual correctness : the gender-feminist attack on women / by
Wendy McElroy.
      p. cm.
    Includes bibliographical references and index.
    ISBN 0-7864-0226-1 (library binding : 50# alk. paper) ∞
    1. Feminism—United States.   2. Feminist theory—United States.
3. Political correctness—United States. I. Title.
HQ1421.M34   1996
305.42—dc20   96-25691
                                                    CIP

Manufactured in the United States of America

McFarland & Company, Inc., Publishers
  Box 611, Jefferson, North Carolina 28640

To Robert Kephart and his inexhaustible
faith in new writers. Thanks Bob.

Contents

THE IDEOLOGIES OF FEMINISM

Gender Feminism: the ideology that views men and women as separate and antagonistic classes. Men oppress women. They do so through the twin evils of the patriarchal state and the free-market system. The goal is not equality: it is gender (class) justice for women.

> *The first theme is the analysis that the social relation between the sexes is organized so that men may dominate and women must submit and this relation is sexual—in fact, is sex.* —Catharine MacKinnon

Liberal Feminism: an ideology in transition. In the '60s it was committed to idea of legal and social equality between the sexes. Since then it has drifted toward the idea of social equity, which often requires granting women legal privileges, such as those contained in affirmative action programs.

Individualist Feminism: an ideology based on the principle "a woman's body, a woman's right." It makes no distinction between civil and economic liberty, between a woman's right to pose for pornography and to act as a surrogate mother. Both are matters of contract and consent. Government—the institutionalization of force—is seen as the greatest threat to women's freedom.

> *To me, any dependence, any thing which destroys the complete self-hood of the individual, is in the line of slavery.* —Voltairine de Cleyre

Preface

Sexual Correctness sketches a new ideological paradigm for feminism—individualist feminism—through analyzing a wide range of gender-related current issues. This goal involves critiquing the existing paradigm, but my criticisms are not meant to harm the feminist movement. Quite the contrary. I believe that feminism as we know it in the 1990s is in danger of calcifying into dogma that is stifling the voices of women who dissent. I fear that feminism may be on the verge of harming women.

My broad focus requires that I touch only lightly on many subjects that deserve a far more detailed analysis. It is my intention to correct this by developing book length treatments of several of these topics. My 1995 book *XXX: A Woman's Right to Pornography* is an in-depth examination of pornography and my forthcoming book *Gutter Feminism* is a presentation of the prostitutes' rights movement in the United States.

Apologies are due to 50 percent of the human race: that is, to men. In analyzing issues from rape to sexual harassment to prostitution, I speak as though they affect only women. This is an artificial limitation which I imposed upon the book because of space constraints and a desire to streamline an already complex presentation of ideas. As I said, my apologies.

I wish to thank Robert Kephart, Andrea Millen Rich of Laissez-Faire Books, and David Boaz of the Cato Institute for enabling a grant from the Roy Childs Fund under which this book was written. Thanks are also due to the Institute for Humane Studies, which financed the bibliographic essay that appears at the conclusion.

Many people were generous with their input and encouragement. In particular, I am grateful to the many sex workers who filled out my surveys and answered pages of questions that may have seemed rather academic. Special thanks are extended to the heads of COYOTE, Norma

Almodovar, Catherine La Croix, and Priscilla Alexander, for facilitating the anonymous mailing. Dozens of women and men involved in pornography took the time to give me a realistic sense of their profession. In particular, I extend my thanks to Nina Hartley, Bobby Lilly, Candida Royalle of Femme Productions, Kat Sunlove of the *Spectator*, Brenda Tatelbaum of *Eidos*, John Stagliano and Phil Harvey.

Nadine Strossen, president of the ACLU, was unstinting in her enthusiasm and support. Joan Taylor Kennedy, president of the Association of Libertarian Feminists, provided much needed perspective. Sharon Presley, the founder of ALF, patiently delineated fine lines of disagreement. *Liberty* magazine and its sharp-eyed staff provided a valuable testing ground for many of the themes and theories that were later woven into this book. Nick Gillespie at *Reason* magazine worked with me on an article which later gave birth to the chapter on reproductive technology.

Within the text itself, I have attempted to note the many women from whom I have drawn ideas in the belief that they deserve not only gratitude, but credit.

CHAPTER 1

Sexual Correctness

The feminism of the 1960s produced a sexual revolution, and an explosion of choices for women resulted. The feminism of the 1990s has created an orthodoxy, which presents women as victims of patriarchy who must be protected from making wrong choices. Feminism has gone from sexual liberation to sexual correctness, from the politics of equality to the politics of revenge. This chapter gives a critical overview of this ideological shift and lays the groundwork for an issue by issue examination of how sexual correctness is destroying the freedom of women to choose.

Backlash

According to a February 1992 poll conducted by Time/CNN, 63 percent of women do not consider themselves to be feminists. Over the last decade, a rift has grown between feminists and the mainstream of women. Millions of women are defining their lives in nonfeminist terms and are choosing to pursue the satisfactions of domestic life rather than those of a career. Even successful business women shy away from the term "feminist."

Contemporary feminist literature—from Susan Faludi's scholarly *Backlash* to Gloria Steinem's more personal autobiography—has attempted to explain why feminism is being marginalized by women. Some of these explanations have come close to condemning any woman who diverges from the feminist agenda. Consider, for example, the issue of pornography. In the anthology *Sexual Liberals and the Attack on Feminism*, the editor Dorchen Leidholdt claims that fellow feminists who say that women in the porn industry have chosen to be there are spreading "a felicitous lie." Contributor Andrea Dworkin states that feminists who defend pornography—even purely on the basis of free speech—are guilty of running a "sex protection racket." She maintains that no one making such a defense can be a feminist. Contributor Wendy Stock accuses pro-porn feminists of identifying with their oppressors "much like ... concentration camp prisoners with their jailers."[1]

In feminist circles it has become popular to claim that the movement is actually *not* on the decline but is merely experiencing a backlash. Indeed, feminists argue that this backlash is a sign of feminism's great strength, since the powers that be obviously feel threatened enough to retaliate. There may be some truth to this, but the theory—at least, as it is presented—is not provable. And feminism does itself no favor by refusing to deal straight-out with criticism.

One of the reasons so many women no longer consider themselves feminists is that the movement has dramatically changed over the last two decades. It no longer provides an ideologically comfortable home for many women who would otherwise call themselves feminists.

Background of Change

The feminist movement of the '90s may seem to be a continuation of '60s feminism. Some of the same voices can still be heard, that of Gloria Steinem, for example. But many of the founding mothers—including Betty Friedan—have become critics of the contemporary movement. Why? What has changed?

In essence, a new ideology has come to the forefront. Modern feminism has always drawn heavily upon the ideology of the left, even down to the terms it uses (e.g., exploitation, gender/class oppression). But the political slant of the mainstream of '60s feminism was liberal. Radical, or gender, feminism was in the political background of the movement.

During the '70s, while mainstream feminists pursued the ERA and secured abortion rights, gender feminists were hammering out a new ideology that comprehensively addressed the condition of women. Gender feminists concluded that all of the ills afflicting women—from date rape to the wage gap, from pornography to sexual harassment—have a common cause. They all flow from patriarchy, especially as it is expressed through the white-male system of capitalism. Gender theorist Adrienne Rich defines patriarchy as

> the power of the fathers: a familial—social, ideological, political system in which men—by force, direct pressure, or through ritual, tradition, law,

and language, customs, etiquette, education, and the division of labor ... [and] in which the female is everywhere subsumed under the male.[2]

With the foundations of ideology carefully laid, gender feminism emerged from the background and moved into the forefront of the movement. As its theories have trickled down and been applied to specific issues, the face of feminism began to alter. It has now changed almost beyond recognition. It has gone from liberalism to political correctness, from a demand for equality to a cry for privilege.

Consider how the movement's attitude toward men has changed. In the '60s and '70s feminists blasted men for viewing women as sex objects and domestic slaves. Men were admonished to show more sensitivity and to share equally in activities such as parenting. They were handed dish towels and pointedly advised to do their share of housework. The quintessential liberal, Alan Alda, appeared on the cover of women's magazines as the ideal "new" man: caring, supportive, and a tad androgynous.

By the '80s and '90s gender feminists had redefined the movement's view of the opposite sex. Men, as a class, were no longer considered reformable. Andrea Dworkin pronounced *all* men to be rapists. Catharine MacKinnon said that marriage, rape, and prostitution are indistinguishable from each other. Kate Millett called for the end of the family unit. A hot anger toward men seems to have turned into a cold hatred.

In the '60s and '70s liberal feminists had embraced sexual liberation. Women had been chafing at the sexual restrictions of the 1950s with dictates that included: no intercourse before marriage, no children out of wedlock, and, certainly, no lesbianism. With sexual liberation, women blossomed. They attended classes on how to masturbate and achieve orgasms; their curiosity led them to consume pornography in increasing numbers; they obtained access to abortion on demand; birth control became widely available; couples lived together openly; lesbians marched arm in arm down the streets; and single motherhood became an acceptable option.

In the '80s and '90s gender feminists defined pornography, in and of itself, as an act of violence against all women. Prostitution became an act of capitalist exploitation. The new reproductive technologies, such as in vitro fertilization, were attacked as medicalized violence on the bodies of women. Open discussions of sex faltered.

In the '60s and '70s women had banged on the doors of business and demanded to be admitted on an equal footing with men. They wanted to be judged solely on the basis of their merits. In the '80s and '90s gender feminists have explicitly rejected equality and clamored for privilege, demanding access to jobs on the basis of gender and on the grounds of having been discriminated against for centuries. A call for reform has become a cry for revolution.

And somewhere along the line the rebellious joy has drained out of the feminist movement. Instead of celebrating the pleasures of sex, women are now barraged only by its perils: rape, domestic violence, harassment. Instead of discussing how to make marriages into equal partnerships, marriage itself is defined as oppression, and there are endless tragic tales of domestic violence and incest. Helen Reddy's song "I Am Woman ... Watch Me Grow" had been the anthem of liberal feminists because it celebrated the power and determination of women. Now, however, women are defined as victims of oppression. Gone is the emphasis on independence and spunk. Founding feminist Betty Friedan has pleaded for feminism to

> transcend sexual politics and anger against men to express a new vision of family and community. We must go from wallowing in the victim's state to mobilizing the new power of women and men for a larger political agenda on the priorities of life. We're at a dangerous time.[3]

A certain go-to-hell spirit has been replaced by a life-is-hell attitude, and with it a strange new puritanism has gripped the feminist movement. Aberrant sexual views, such as the enjoyment of or indifference to pornography, will not be tolerated. The repressive attitudes have emanated from the left wing of the movement, which has had an influence far out of proportion to the actual number of gender feminists occupying that end of the spectrum. Their influence has been augmented by another relatively new force on the political scene: the political correctness movement.

Political and Sexual Correctness

Gender feminism has joined hands with political correctness—a movement that condemns the panorama of western civilization as sexist and racist: the product of "dead white males." Those who are politically correct champion categories of people who have been historically victimized by white males. In other words, women and minorities.

Gender feminists demand that to redress the past injustice against women present-day white males become sexually correct. Sexual correctness is an all-embracing theory dictating how husbands should treat wives, what comments strangers on the street may make to women passing by, how much employers should pay female workers, what subjects coworkers may discuss, and how women may use their own bodies (e.g., not posing for pornographic pictures).

In the personal realm sexual correctness has redefined, collectivized, and politicized the crime of rape. It is no longer a crime between individuals. It is a political act that men, as a class, commit against women, as a class. In the business world, it has sparked laws against sexual harassment. In essence, the First Amendment no longer applies to the workplace.

Centuries ago a righteous persecution of "bad" religious attitudes was conducted by the Catholic Church: the Inquisition. A righteous persecution of "bad" sexual attitudes is now in progress. Bad attitudes toward women are no longer merely boorish; they are also legally actionable. To avoid prosecution, business, government, and academia are imposing de facto quota systems and sexual codes upon themselves. The reasons for this compliance are clear. In a recent sex discrimination case against the University of Minnesota, the attorney's fees alone amounted to $1,475,000. (The plaintiff later quit academia to become a lawyer.) Under these circumstances, who can afford to be right?

On a more individual level, men are afraid to pay female coworkers a compliment lest it be called harassment, and they mutter to each other that promotions are now a matter of gender, not merit. The myth of sleeping one's way to the top has been replaced with the unpleasant possibility of suing one's way into that position.

As political correctness has grown in influence, there has been an increase in the resentment directed by men against women. This is inevitable. Any movement that condemns a whole class of people, such as white males, as oppressors with no reference to the obvious fairness and compassion of so many individuals within that class, is almost certain to produce hostility. And, indeed, the goal of gender feminism is nothing short of violent conflict. Revolution requires such methods. Sexual correctness can only exacerbate hostility toward women and so increase the injustice they suffer. In his book *Illiberal Education*, Dinesh D'Souza makes the sad comment that this hostility is "prejudice, not from ignorance, but from experience."

So far, social institutions and the business world seem to have approached sexual correctness with a strategy of reluctant accommodation. This strategy is not working, and it can never work for the reason that gender feminists are not asking for fair or equal treatment within the present system. They are demanding the elimination of the present system, which is defined as inherently and irredeemably unjust. They are calling for revolution, and no amount of reform will do.

Andrea Dworkin—one of the loudest voices for sexual correctness— explains the revolutionary nature of this agenda: "In order to stop ... systematic abuses against us, we must destroy these very definitions of masculinity and femininity, of men and women." Dworkin continues by outlining precisely what must be eradicated in our society:

> We must destroy the very structure of culture as we know it, its art, its churches, its laws; we must eradicate from consciousness and memory all of the images, institutions, and structural mental sets that turn men into rapists by definition and women into victims by definition.[4]

The feminist movement has shifted from a desire for equal treatment within the system to a demand to "destroy the very structure of culture as we know it." An important step in this ideological shift came in 1970. In that year, Kate Millett's pivotal book, *Sexual Politics*, appeared: it advanced the idea that sexual relations are political. In that same year, Shulamith Firestone's *The Dialectic of Sex* urged women "to develop a materialist view of history based on sex itself." Gender feminists rushed to do so. The most prominent analysis remains Susan Brownmiller's *Against Our Will* (1975), which defined rape as a political crime and "gave it its history."

To paraphrase a popular slogan of the '70s: "the personal became political." Complex connections were drawn between everyday personal encounters and the brutalization of women through rape and assault. British feminists began complaining about the tendency of British men to call them "love." American feminists decried the Southern habit of calling women "honey." The reasoning behind the uproar was that such men, through these small, relatively inoffensive acts, contribute to a social and sexual environment that makes rape not only possible, but politically inevitable.

Rape has become a standard weapon of male oppression. The title of a recent book from gender feminism assures women that we live in a "rape culture." There is no other way to protect defenseless women, we are told, than to vigorously stamp out all attitudes that sustain rape. This vigilance has produced new categories of crime, such as sexual harassment. Sex and all other personal or business relationships have come under a political/sexual microscope. They have become part of a gender agenda.

Sexual correctness is the banner under which gender feminists are waging war against the twin enemies of patriarchy and capitalism. Of patriarchy, Dworkin writes:

Under patriarchy, every woman is a victim, past, present, and future. Under patriarchy, every woman's daughter is a victim, past, present, and future. Under patriarchy, every women's son is her potential betrayer and also the inevitable rapist or exploiter of another woman.[5]

On capitalism, gender feminist Heidi Gottfried comments:

Male violence against women represents a regular feature of male domination throughout history and under capitalism and constitutes a mechanism of social control.... In addition to an economic basis for the perpetuation of sexual coercion, violence reinforces women's economic dependence on a male wage.[6]

To these feminists, the enemy is the class who ultimately benefits from patriarchy and capitalism: men, especially white men. Not the individual man who actually rapes and batters a woman, but men as a class. *All* males are oppressors, because maleness in and of itself is violence against women. Viewed through this political lens, maleness is not even a biological trait; it is a cultural one. The sexually correct lawyer Catharine MacKinnon insists, "Male is a social and political concept, not a biological attribute."[7] Thus, men are not considered as individuals, but as a gender class.

Dworkin expands on the new meaning of maleness:

The very identity of men, their civil and economic power, the forms of government that they have developed, the wars they wage are tied *irrevocably* together. All forms of dominance and submission ... are tied *irrevocably* to the sexual identities of men and are derived from the male sexual model.[8]

Not surprisingly the rejection of maleness borders on a rejection of heterosexuality itself. MacKinnon comments on heterosexual sex, "If there is no inequality, no violation, no dominance, no force, there is no sexual arousal."[9]

Gender Feminist Methodology

Gender feminism's attack on patriarchy has not been an overwhelming success. The vast majority of women withdraw from an ideology that requires them to denounce their infant sons as natural rapists. After all, most women still consider themselves heterosexual; they choose to marry; they love their male offspring; they may even enjoy traditional sex.

Gender feminists dismiss such women as "unawakened." In her

article, *P.C. or B.S.?*, Meredith McGhan describes the response that a sexually correct professor offered to the liberal feminist Christina Hoff Sommers, who objected to such a cavalier dismissal of women's self-perception:

> Sommers pointed out that many women did not feel oppressed in their chosen roles as wife and mother, and that some even enjoyed wearing makeup and fashionable clothing. "Thanks a *lot*, Christina," [the professor] later said, rolling his eyes, implying that Sommers had done a real disservice to women everywhere.[10]

Anyone with intellectual honesty must credit empirical evidence and the demonstrated preferences of hundreds of millions of women. Anyone with objectivity must admit that marriage exists because it offers many women something they want. That is why they choose it.

A key to the amazing facility with which gender feminists dismiss such evidence lies in what has been called "feminist methodology." This is a revolutionary new approach to research. Because logic and the scientific method are considered to be traditional white male methods, gender feminists reject them as oppressive. They evolve their own oppression-free methodology. In a recent issue of *American Scholar*, Margarita Levin explained how even physical laws are being rejected as "masculine." Ms. Levin writes:

> [Feminist scientists] see male dominance at work in, for instance, the "master molecule" theory of DNA functioning; in the notion of forces "acting on" objects; in the description of evolution as the result of a "struggle" to survive; in the view that scarcity of resources results in "competition" between animals.

Ms. Levin reveals the underlying theme of the new feminist methodology: "in short in any theory positing what they deem destructive, violent, unidirectional, or hierarchical.... The idea of dominance is directly linked to the notion of scientific objectivity."[11]

Feminist methodology stresses the importance of women's personal experiences. For example, interviewing women is called "the politics of experience," and it is a mainstay of feminist research. The personal approach has a myriad of problems—over and above a total lack of objectivity. For one thing, gender feminists interview and credit only those women who have been victimized and who consider themselves to be oppressed by men. The experiences of women who have not been abused or who consider most men to be fellow travelers are entirely ignored. The antipornography crusader Catharine MacKinnon, for example, refuses to debate or publicly discuss pornography with women who disagree with her stand. She has ignored repeated calls from Nadine Strossen, president of the ACLU, to have an open forum.

Equally, there have been few attempts to do serious research on men, who constitute fully one half of the perceived problem. Indeed, gender feminists adamantly refuse to credit the voices of men. It is difficult to understand how a balanced picture could emerge from such flawed research.

Perhaps the most blatant example of poor methodology comes as part and parcel of a relatively new issue within feminism: that of suppressed memories. These are memories that are said to be so painful that they have been repressed and only come to the surface years later. The phenomenon is called Recovered Memory Syndrome. Typically, the content of these memories revolves around incest, childhood molestation, or rape. Feminists insist that repressed memories should be treated as "facts." Indeed, such "evidence" is now being used in lawsuits.

But memory, at the best of times, is unreliable. Women who have recalled blocked memories must ask themselves: even if I remember an incident clearly, how do I know that I am not remembering it only so far as I am able to handle the trauma? Or only in terms I can deal with? After all, the memories are so painful that they have been screened out in their entirety for years. In honesty a woman must ask herself, How do I know that my memory is not playing similar tricks now?

Such memories are not necessarily false, but usually they are not verifiable. This means they cannot be used to prove anything else or to support any conclusions. Yet gender feminists rely on precisely such emotionally charged and slanted research. Gender feminists often back up their arguments with a statement akin to "many studies have proven." References and contexts are generally absent. At other times, the flaws in sympathetic research work are simply ignored.

For example, Menachem Amir's interesting study, *Patterns in Forcible Rape* (1971), is often quoted by gender feminists as being "definitive." It supports their view of what rape is. In fact, Amir's study has been the target of considerable criticism outside of the feminist community. Some of the criticisms are fairly minor: figures in tables are transposed, columns fail to add up correctly to the sums indicated, etc. Some of the criticisms, however, are serious enough to call the study into question; for example, Amir based his research on police records, which had many gaps in them. And nowhere did he make it clear that police data must be viewed and used with great caution: police records are compiled for a totally different purpose than sociology. The data has not benefited from any of the screening or safeguards that would accompany a valid study. Nor did Amir include information on reported rapes that had been dismissed by the police. These are reports that failed to convince the police that a crime had occurred or that a conviction could be obtained. Perhaps the report was made by a victim whom the police refused to take seriously—a prostitute or a drug addict, for example.

Yet, in *Against Our Will*, Susan Brownmiller's criticisms of Amir's study seem limited to comments about how "annoyingly obtuse [it was] about the culturally conditioned behavior of women in situations involving force."[12] In other words, it did not go far enough in the direction she favors. She quotes Amir's study extensively as proof of many "facts" that support her theory.

In truth, investigation into most feminist issues is still in its infancy. Studies conflict and intellectual brawls are breaking out even over what questions should be asked. In the introduction to the anthology *Forcible Rape*, Gilbert Geis observes that dispute still surrounds even the simplest of questions regarding rape: for example, whether it can be correlated with any season or period of time:

> Early research seemed to have established beyond equivocation that forcible rape and warm weather were positively related.... Such entrenched wisdom is challenged in this volume, however, when Chappell and Singer reported that forcible rape in New York City reaches its numerical peak during the winter months.[13]

Feminist research is so new that it should be exploding in all directions; instead, it is calcifying into dogma. Gender feminists insist that they have the "definitive" and only answer. By viciously attacking those who question their data or conclusions, gender feminists do women a grave disservice. They stifle discussion; they discourage the emergence of truth.

Bad data and bad research can only produce more myths about subjects such as rape and domestic violence. Misusing studies and statistics, however, is not unique to gender feminism. What is unique is the extent to which their methodology explicitly abandons objectivity in preference for subjectivity. Objectivity is abandoned in the name of ideology. The specific ideology adopted by these sexually correct women is quasi–Marxist: they consider patriarchy, as expressed through capitalism, to be the primary means by which white male society oppresses women.

At some point, a gender feminist with any honesty must confront a moral dilemma. What about women who do not interpret their experiences in the same ideological terms as she does? What of the women who look at the same society and interpret it differently? Should gender feminists take a lesson from white males and impose their own reality upon "erring" women? Should they apply their gender theories like a politically correct grid over the protests of unawakened women? If so, what happens to the oft stated ideal of valuing the experiences of women?

To phrase the question differently: when the experiences of real women conflict with gender feminist theory, which one wins out? The answer is clear. Gender feminists dismiss inconvenient real-world experiences and people. They do not credit, for example, the voices of prostitutes in COYOTE,[14] who are outspoken in defense of their occupation. They do not respect the experiences of women in the porn industry, who argue in favor of graphic sexual expression. Gender feminists simply ignore women who do not view patriarchy as a source of oppression. Such women are said to be misinterpreting their own lives. They desperately need to be politically awakened because have been brainwashed by the "world of men."

To dismiss so cavalierly the voices of women who dissent is a slap in the face of every woman. To present a view of women as weak-willed and feeble-minded in the face of patriarchy is an insult to our sex. It is patronizing and disrespectful; it is a form of mental abuse. No wonder feminists are often despised by sex workers. But what specifically is the ideology that leads gender feminists to dismiss the voices of sexually incorrect women?

The Ideology of Gender Feminism

Catharine MacKinnon calls it "post–Marxism." The modifier "post" is inserted because a certain tension exists between feminism and Marxism, which stems largely from the different ways these two theories approach class analysis.

A class is nothing more than a category of things or people sharing one or more characteristics. The characteristic(s) can be anything: height, weight, religion, sex. The person doing research or forming a theory picks out whatever characteristic is considered to be significant for his or her purpose. The purpose of gender feminists is political. They have chosen sex as the politically most significant characteristic of human beings. Accordingly, their political theory classifies the world along the lines of gender. By contrast, Marxists consider the most important political characteristic to be the relationship of each person to the mode of production. They classify human beings according to whether they are workers or capitalists.

To ascertain what is just, gender feminism asks only, What sex are you? It does not ask Are you a worker or a capitalist? In its scheme of justice, Marxism asks only, Are you a worker or a capitalist? It does not care what sex a person is. In other words, Marxism does not recognize the political significance of feminist issues, such as date rape, pornography, and abortion. Catharine MacKinnon explains nicely the rift between these two ideologies. She writes, "Sexuality is to feminism what work is to Marxism."[15] MacKinnon then attempts to resolve this tension by evolving the political theory she calls post–Marxist feminism:

> As an example of post–Marxist feminism, I want to consider the often-raised question of whether "all women" are oppressed by heterosexuality.... If you applied such an analysis to the issue of work ... would you agree, as people say about heterosexuality, that a worker chooses to work?

MacKinnon continues by postulating a situation in which working conditions are very good and the workers are happy. Does this change the fact that they are exploited? MacKinnon extends this to become a metaphor for women who seem happy in motherhood and marriage: "If you even like your work, or have a good day at work, does that mean, from a Marxist perspective, your work is not exploited? Those who think that one chooses heterosexuality ... should either explain why it is not compulsory or explain why the word choice can be meaningful here."[16]

How is the inequality of women to be explained? MacKinnon explains elsewhere: "Feminism needs to create an entirely new account of the political world. Feminism thus stands in relation to Marxism as Marxism does to classical political economy: its final conclusion and ultimate critique."[17]

Marxism and feminism are both theories of the distribution of political power. Post–Marxist feminists propose to distribute power, not through equality, but through their vision of social justice. That is, they do not seek equality under the law but a total restructuring of the law itself and of the system creating the law. They seek to impose sexually correct attitudes and behavior in both the economic and the personal realm. And the success of their campaign has been partly due to the strategy they have adopted.

Gender Feminist Strategy

For the last decade, gender feminists have used the civil courts as a means of implementing their political agenda. The groundwork for this strategy was laid by liberal feminists. For example, with affirmative action, women have sued for unfair employment practices under Title VII of the Civil Rights Act of 1964. The Equal Employment Opportunity Commission (EEOC) has also ruled that sexual harassment is a violation of Title VII and that employers are to be held legally responsible.

More recently, gender feminists have tried to define pornography as discrimination against women in order to pass antiporn ordinances. The first significant attempt at such a measure was the Minneapolis Anti-Pornography Ordinance of 1983. Andrea Dworkin and Catharine MacKinnon were hired as consultants by conservative city legislators who wished to clean the streets of pornography.

The Minneapolis ordinance was drafted as a civil rights law. It would have given individual women, or groups of women, the right to take producers or distributors of pornography to civil court for damages. The charge would have been "coercing the plaintiff(s) into pornography." That is, forcing women to participate in pornography without their consent.

What constituted consent? The ordinance listed thirteen conditions that were not considered evidence of agreement. A woman could subsequently sue a magazine like *Playboy* even though she had been of age when she posed, had signed a contract and release, had been fully informed of the intent of the photos, received payment, had been under no threat, and had displayed no resistance. In essence, the ordinance obviated the possibility of a woman consenting to pornography.

Recently, through the Violence Against Women Act (VAWA), gender feminists have opened the door to using civil courts to address issues such as rape. The VAWA was part of the voluminous Crime Act that was passed in 1994 with very few people knowing its full contents.

The strategy of ordinances and civil suits has many advantages. It can be executed on a city by city or case by case basis. The fight can be localized and score victories in sympathetic venues, which may then serve as legal precedents. This strategy also avoids the need to obtain a national consensus, which proved so difficult with the ERA. Moreover, civil courts are less stringent than criminal ones. The rules of evidence are relaxed. Women are not subjected to severe cross-examination. Convicting someone in criminal court requires evidence "beyond a reasonable doubt," which is often defined as 99 percent certainty. Civil court requires only a preponderance of the evidence, which can be 51 percent certainty.

The main advantage of this strategy to gender feminists, however, is that they can hitch their own political agenda onto established and venerated pieces of legislation—such as the Civil Rights Act. If feminist issues can be shifted into the arena of civil rights, the battle is half won.

In his essay, *Race Unconsciousness and the White Male*, Frederick R. Lynch comments on "the quiet, behind-the-scenes fashion in which judges and administrators formulated and implemented affirmative action." His words apply also to an ever wider range of feminist issues: "In effect, an old Marxist slogan has been updated for contemporary social policy: from each according to his/her ability, to each according to his/her ethnicity or gender.... Corporate capitalist culture has become 'white male culture.'"[18]

Individualist Feminism

What can be done to halt the juggernaut of sexual correctness? An idea can be defeated only by a better idea. The ideology of gender feminism can be confronted effectively only by another "radical" and more effective ideology: that of individualist feminism.

Self-ownership is the defining term of individualist feminism. It is the conviction that every human being has moral jurisdiction over his or her own body. Women, as human beings, have exactly the same rights and political interests as men do. The right is self-ownership; the political interest is freedom. And the most fundamental of these shared rights is the ability to control one's own body and peaceful actions. To claim that someone else has jurisdiction over one's body is to argue for slavery. The goal of self-ownership is equality under laws that embody individual rights.

The nineteenth-century individualist feminist Voltairine de Cleyre expressed the ideology well when she wrote, "To me, any dependence, any thing which destroys the complete selfhood of the individual, is in the line of slavery."[19]

The "complete selfhood" of which de Cleyre writes is embodied in "choice," as the nineteenth-century individualist feminist Lillian Harman knew well. At the age of sixteen, Lillian was imprisoned for defying the marriage laws of Kansas. She broke the law deliberately in order to encourage a legal redefinition of marriage, which would bring greater freedom for women. In arguing for a diversity of attitudes and choices, Harman wrote:

I consider uniformity in mode of sexual relations as undesirable and impractical as enforced uniformity in anything else. For myself, I want the right to profit by my mistakes ... and why should I be unwilling for others to enjoy the same liberty? If I should be able to bring the entire world to live exactly as I live at present, what would that avail me in ten years, when as I hope, I shall have a broader knowledge of life, and my life therefore probably changed.[20]

In at least one sense gender and individualist feminism have more in common with each other than they do with mainstream, or liberal, feminism. They both want radical change, whereas liberals seek reform. In general, liberal feminists want equal representation and fair treatment within the existing system, e.g., more women elected to Congress. Both gender and individualist feminists claim that the existing system is a source of injustice and must be redesigned. Gender feminists want the new system to be an expression of collective justice and proper economic distribution. Individualist feminists want full protection of their self-ownership.

The roots of individualist feminism are deep within the heart of the American tradition. Feminism itself, as an organized movement, arose from abolitionism in the early 1830s. Abolitionism was the radical anti-slavery movement that demanded the immediate cessation of slavery on the grounds that every man was a self-owner. It was the first American political movement in which women played prominent roles as organizers, writers, and lecturers. As they argued for the self-ownership of black men, women within abolitionism were naturally inclined to ask, What of women? Are we not self-owners as well?

In 1840 Wm. Garrison and several female abolitionists journeyed to the World Anti-Slavery Conference in London. When the less enlightened British conference refused to seat women in the main assembly, Garrison—now classified as a "dead white male"—walked out in protest. Eight years later, the Seneca Falls Convention was organized by women who had experienced that slap in the face. During the first Seneca Falls Convention a women's suffrage resolution was introduced: "Resolved, that it is the duty of the women in this country to secure to themselves their sacred right to the elective franchise."[21] For decades thereafter, mainstream feminists were consumed with the goal of suffrage. They were consumed by a passion for equal representation within the system.

Meanwhile, socialist feminists—the American forerunners of gender feminism—pushed for social reforms, such as the Pure Food Act and child labor laws. Individualist feminists aimed, not at social purity, but at the freedom to use their own bodies as they saw fit. They fought for birth control and the reform of marriage laws. Most of their work was done in the pages of currently obscure periodicals, such as *Lucifer the Light Bearer*, *Liberty*, and *The Word*.[22] Indeed, *The Word* contains the earliest appeal I have ever seen for open abortion, based on the argument "it is a woman's body, it is a woman's right." It was written by the individualist Angela Heywood, whose husband, Ezra, was repeatedly imprisoned under the Comstock Laws for dispensing birth control information.

Perhaps the best way to illustrate the difference between gender and individualist feminism is not through a discussion of their theory or history but through a presentation of how each ideology deals with the specific issues of modern feminism. This is what the following chapters aim to accomplish.

Notes

1. Dorchen Leidholdt and Janice G. Raymond, eds., *Sexual Liberals and the Attack on Feminism* (New York: Pergamon Press, 1990), pp. 131, 136, 150.

2. Adrienne Rich, *Of Woman Born: Motherhood as Experience and Institution* (London: Virago, 1977), p. 57.

3. *Time*, March 1992.

4. Andrea Dworkin, *Our Blood: Prophecies and Discourses on Sexual Politics* (New York: Harper & Row, 1976), p. 48.

5. Ibid., p. 20.

6. Heidi Gottfried, "Preventing Sexual Coercion: A Feminist Agenda for Economic Change," in *Sexual Coercion: A Sourcebook on Its Nature, Causes, and Prevention*, ed. Elizabeth Grauerholz and Mary A. Koralewski (Lexington, Mass.: Lexington, 1991), p. 175.

7. Catharine A. MacKinnon, *Toward a Feminist Theory of the State* (Cambridge, Mass.: Harvard University Press, 1987), p. 114.

8. Dworkin, *Our Blood*, p. 11.

9. Quoted in James R. Petersen, "Catharine MacKinnon: Again," *Playboy*, August 1992, pp. 37–39.

10. Meredith McGhan "P.C. or B.S.?" in *Liberty* (4) (March 1992): 31–32.

11. As quoted in *National Review*, November 18, 1991, p. 32.

12. Susan Brownmiller, *Against Our Will: Men, Women, and Rape*, (New York: Bantam Books, 1976), p. 180.

13. Gil Geis "Introduction," in *Forcible Rape: The Crime, the Victim, and the Offender*, ed. Duncan Chappell (New York: Columbia University Press, 1977), p. 23.

14. COYOTE (Call Off Your Old Tired Ethics) is a national sex worker advocacy group in America.

15. Catharine A. MacKinnon, *Feminism Unmodified: Discourses on Life and Law* (Cambridge, Mass.: Harvard University Press, 1987), p. 48.

16. MacKinnon, *Feminism Unmodified*, p. 60.

17. MacKinnon, *Toward a Feminist Theory of the State*, p. 125.

18. *Society*, January/February 1992.

19. As quoted in *Freedom, Feminism, and the State: An Overview of Individualist*

Feminism, ed. Wendy McElroy, rev. ed. (New York: Holmes & Meier, 1991), p. 35.

20. Ibid., p. 16.

21. Susan B. Anthony, Elizabeth Cady Stanton, and Ida H. Harper, *The History of Woman Suffrage*, vol 1 (New York: Fowler & Wells, 1881–1922), pp. 70–73.

22. Please see chapter 12, "A Brief Bibliographical Essay," for more information on these periodicals.

CHAPTER TWO

The New Mythology of Rape

Destroying the Old Mythology

The word "rape" comes from the Latin *rapere*, which means to "take by force." And taking women by force is one issue on which all feminists should agree. Rape is an abomination that no civilized society can tolerate. In the '60s liberal feminists broke down the mythology of rape that had been built up by a puritanical and sexist culture. They shattered the presumption that only "bad" girls who walked alone at night were raped. Research showed exactly the opposite to be true. Every woman, from infancy to the grave, was vulnerable to attack, even in her own home and especially from the men she knew. Liberal feminists exploded the myth that rapists were seedy men who lurked in alleys. Some offenders *were* hardened criminals and psychopaths, but research revealed that many rapists were fathers, husbands, and even the apple-cheeked boy who lives next door.

Liberal feminists attacked a court system that believed rape complainants were less reliable than other victims. Until the 1970s, many states advised juries to be cautious about accepting the testimony of a rape victim who was "unchaste." Moreover, most states recognized a "reasonable resistance" requirement; that is, rape was not deemed to have occurred unless the woman had manifested genuine resistance. No other crime required a victim to resist in order to prove a crime had occurred.

In the 1970s feminists crusaded to reform rape laws in order to drop the resistance requirement and to eliminate any investigation into whether the rape complainant was "unchaste." In 1986 the California Supreme Court ruled that physical resistance was not necessary for rape to have occurred. The past sexual experience of rape complainants is now generally considered inadmissible in court.

As the mythology of rape crumbled, feminism replaced it with facts and with practical help for women in pain. The first rape crisis line in the United States was established in 1971. These rape hotlines and crisis centers did something the legal system and research could not: they talked to raped women and helped them to make it through one more night.

As a woman who was raped, I owe a debt to '60s feminism. I emerged from the experience in one piece largely because of the groundwork feminism had already laid for rape victims. Periodicals and television shows told me I had the right to be angry, not only at the man who raped me, but also at the laws and cultural attitudes that sheltered him and not me. From feminism I learned an irreplaceable and healing lesson: it was not my fault.

In her book, *Rape on Trial*, Zsuzsanna Adler aptly commented: "It is fitting that the 'rediscovery' of rape should coincide with the growth of the women's movement. Prominent feminists and leading feminist publications have authored or printed many of the relevant writings on the subject."[1]

Creating New Myths

> "Politically, I call it rape whenever a woman has sex and *feels* violated." [Emphasis added.]
>
> Catharine MacKinnon[2]

In the past two decades, a disturbing change has taken place in feminism's approach to rape. Rape used to be considered as an experience different from normal life: a crime, a violation of normal life. But in the 70's theoretical groundwork was laid that placed rape at the very heart of our culture. Rape became an expression of how the average man viewed the average woman. By the 1980's rape had become thoroughly politicized within feminism; it was now viewed as a major weapon (perhaps *the* major weapon) by which patriarchy kept women in their place.

The opening paragraph of the New York Radical Feminists Manifesto maintains that—through consciousness-raising—this group discovered that "rape is not a personal misfortune but an experience shared by all women in one form or another. When more than two people have suffered the same oppression the problem is no longer personal but political—and rape is a political matter."

The manifesto continues by describing "man's treatment of woman": "He has found ways to enslave her ... as a final proof of his power and her debasement as a possession, a thing, a chunk of meat, he has raped her. The act of rape is the logical expression of the essential relationship now existing between men and women."[3]

Rape was no longer a crime committed by individuals against individuals; it had become part of class analysis. Rape had found its niche within a political ideology with a revolutionary agenda. Susan Griffin expresses the ideological underpinning of this shift in rape theory in her book, *Rape: The Power of Consciousness*. Here, she argues that the true rapist is not the individual man, but the political system of patriarchy:

> From Marxism I had learned a habit of looking for social causes and observing how human nature is shaped by external condition.... But the Left had an ideology, which, beyond and in addition to its prejudice against women, did not agree with the changes we experienced.

Griffin sums up the logical conclusion to the tension between gender feminist and the Left: "We rejected the theory that capitalism had raped us. If they said patriarchy was just a form of capitalism, we said that capitalism was a form of patriarchy."[4] A key philosopher of gender feminism, Adrienne Rich, offered insight into the nature of the source of all rape—patriarchy:

> Patriarchy is the power of the fathers: a familial—social, ideological, political system in which men—by force, direct pressure, or through ritual, tradition, law, and language, customs, etiquette, education, and the division of labor, determine what part women should or shall not play.[5]

Rich concludes that "the female is everywhere subsumed under the male."

Rape became a political accident waiting to happen. This view has gained distressing popularity within feminist circles, where rape has almost ceased to be a crime—like battery or murder—criminals commit against individual women. Now it has been placed at the service of a larger political, social, and economic worldview. It has become an accusation thrown wholesale at white male culture and all men.

In her near-legendary essay, "Rape: The All-American Crime," gender feminist Susan Griffin makes what no longer sounds like such a radical claim:

> Indeed, the existence of rape in any form is beneficial to the ruling class of white males. For rape is a kind of terrorism which severely limits the freedom of women and makes women dependent on men.... This

oppressive attitude towards women finds its institutionalization in the traditional family.[6]

Contra Against Our Will

There is a pivotal point in feminism's shift on the issue of rape. In 1975 the book *Against Our Will* by Susan Brownmiller appeared. In its pages, Brownmiller charts the history of rape from Neanderthal times through to the modern era, placing great emphasis on periods of war and crisis. *Against Our Will* is a watershed book, which was said to "give rape its history." It also presented new theory. Brownmiller maintains that rape is the primary mechanism through which men in general perpetuate their dominance over women in general. She claims that all men benefit from the fact that some men rape.

I understand how compelling this view of rape can be. At times, I have wanted to blame all men for the violence I experienced. Certainly, I was angry at all men. But there are at least two problems with gender feminism's theory of rape. It is wrong. And it is damaging to women.

In the process of politicizing and collectivizing the pain of women, gender feminism is reversing the gains of the '60s—when the myths about rape and the barriers between men and women had a chance of being dissolved. Today, new myths and new barriers are being erected.

Any examination of this new mythology should begin with *Against Our Will*. There, Brownmiller makes three basic and interconnected claims:

1. Rape is a part of patriarchy;
2. Men have created a mass psychology of rape; and,
3. Rape is a part of normal life.

I dispute every one of these claims.

The first new myth Brownmiller advances, that rape is a part of patriarchy, is perhaps the most basic genderfeminist myth about rape, namely, that the crime has one cause, and a political one at that: the general oppression of women by men. Herein lies the extreme interpretation of the slogan "the personal is political."

Against Our Will arrives at this conclusion more as a result of ideological bias than of empirical research. Although Brownmiller's book is sometimes taken for a chronicle of historical fact, a strong political slant underlies the presentation of those facts. Consider Brownmiller's attitude toward private property: "Concepts of hierarchy, slavery, and private property flowed from, and could only be predicated upon, the initial subjugation of woman."[7] And: "Slavery, private property, and the subjugation of women were facts of life, and the earliest written law that has come down to us reflects this stratified life."[8]

To individualist feminists, slavery is not a companion concept for private property. It is the abrogation of the most basic form of private property: self-ownership, that is, of the natural and inalienable claim that all people have to their own bodies. In other words, slavery is *the* most extreme example of the breakdown of private property. And the recognition of private property is women's best defense against rape.

In her book *Sexual Personae*, the individualist Camille Paglia offers a different perspective. Instead of viewing our culture as the cause of rape, Paglia argues that it is the main protection women have against attack. Thus, women can walk down a street unmolested not in spite of society, but because of it. Paglia writes: "Generation after generation, men must be educated, refined, and ethically persuaded away from their tendency toward anarchy and brutishness. Society is not the enemy, as feminism ignorantly claims. Society is woman's protection against rape."[9]

Brownmiller's second claim is that men, in general, have created a mass psychology of rape. Brownmiller claims that all men are rapists at heart and all women their natural prey:

> Man's discovery that his genitalia could serve as a weapon to generate fear must rank as one of the most important discoveries of prehistoric times, along with the use of fire and the first crude stone axe. From prehistoric times to the present, I believe, rape has played a critical function.

Brownmiller concludes that rape "is nothing more or less than a conscious process of intimidation by which *all* men keep *all* women in a state of fear."[10]

Although one might question how Brownmiller comes by her amazing information about rape and male attitudes in prehistoric times, her message is clear. Men are inherently rapists. To back up this statement, Brownmiller plays fast and loose with anecdotal accounts and passages of fiction. The selection of excerpts shows great bias. At one point, Brownmiller notes: "People often ask what the classic Greek myths reveal about rape. Actually, they reveal very little."[11]

Yet these myths are widely held to be archetypes of human psychology. If Brownmiller wishes to maintain that there is a continuum of male oppression—that extends from man's first recognition of his genitalia as weapon through to this moment—she *must*, in honesty, credit Greek myths. She cannot pick and chose only the statistics and anecdotal accounts that support her position. Yet even dipping into history and fiction when and where she chooses, Brownmiller's evidence does not support her conclusion that all men are rapists.

To back this contention, gender feminists have produced truly horrifying statistics. In the preface to their book *Acquaintance Rape: The Hidden Crime*, editors Andrea Parrot and Laurie Bechhofer offer a common statistic: "Approximately one in four women in the United States will be the victims of rape or attempted rape by the time they are in their midtwenties, and over three quarters of those assaults will occur between people who know each other."[12]

This is a stunning figure and one supported by FBI records. In looking at such terrifying statistics, women have a natural tendency to overlook a vital aspect of what is being said. Even accepting the statistics, three out of four women will *not* be raped. Even assuming that there is a one-to-one correlation between victims and rapists—a generous assumption since many rapists commit serial crimes—this means that 75 percent of all men will never commit this brutal crime.

This observation may seem obvious or facile. But in the face of astounding and unsupported claims like "all men are rapists," it becomes necessary to state the obvious. If another group of radicals claimed that "all whites/Protestants/bisexuals are sadists," while their own statistics indicated that 75 percent of the accused group were nonsadists, no honest observer would accept their argument. But because the radicals are sexually correct feminists, their incredible statements are swallowed whole.

And lest a single man slip through the net of accusations by pleading that he had never raped or even contemplated doing so, Brownmiller explains how good intentions and good behavior do not excuse a man from the charge of rape. She freely admits that men: "commit their acts of aggression *without awareness, for the most part, that they have committed a punishable crime,* let alone a moral wrong."[13]

Even seemingly innocent men are guilty because they benefit from the "rape culture." Such a theory allows for no contradictory evidence. There is no possibility—through action, thought, or word—for a man to escape the charge of rape. It becomes axiomatically true.

The third of Brownmiller's claims is that rape is part of normal life. To reach this conclusion, Brownmiller makes great leaps of logic. For example, *Against Our Will* examines rape, primarily during times of war and political crisis. Although this is valuable, Brownmiller pushes her point one step farther. She concludes that—because men rape in times of war and social turbulence—all men are normally rapists. In essence, rape is the norm.

But the very circumstances Brownmiller highlights—war, riots, pogroms, and revolutions—are not so much expressions of society as they are evidence of its breakdown. Yet, in chapter after chapter, Brownmiller uses horrifying accounts of rape during societal breakdowns in order to argue that this is how the man in the street reacts. Arguing from the extreme, Brownmiller draws conclusions about the normal.

There is no doubt: in times of war and social upheaval, the frequency of all violence increases, but this says nothing about the state of regular life. Nor does it indicate whether the violence is caused by society or by the forces destroying society. In essence, Brownmiller's book commits the logical fallacy of generalizing from extreme cases to the norm. But unless one is willing to make statements such as- "men kill in war, therefore the accountant feeding his parking meter during peace time is, by definition, a killer," -one cannot make similar broad statements about rape.

Even when *Against Our Will* moves away from the agonies of war and revolt, it focuses only on situations of polarization and conflict. After the two chapters entitled "War" and "Riots, Pogroms, and Revolutions" comes "Two Studies in American History." These studies involve the history of rape as applied to American Indians and slaves. Again, Brownmiller's insights are valuable.

Again, a leap of logic occurs. Over and over, Brownmiller uses horror stories about, for example, the KKK's persecution of blacks to parallel man's treatment of woman. However emotionally compelling these images might be, they are not arguments, and they do not justify the conclusions she presents.

The Death Knell for Research on Rape

One of the casualties of the new dogma of rape has been research. It is no longer sexually correct to conduct studies on the causes of rape, because—as any right thinking person knows—there is only one cause: patriarchy. Decades ago, during the heyday of liberal feminism and sexual curiosity, the approach to research was more sophisticated.

In his book from the '70s, *Men who Rape: The Psychology of the Offender*, A. Nicholas Groth offers a theory that sounds almost jarring to today's ears: "One of the most basic observations one can make regarding men who rape is that not all such offenders are alike."[14] In their book, *The Crime and Consequences of Rape*, Charles W. Dean, Mary de Bruyn-Kops, and Charles C. Thomas, report: "The Kinsey study, begun in the 1950s and completed after Kinsey's death by Gebhard and associates, classified seven types of rapists: assaultive, amoral, drunken, explosive, double-standard, mental defective and psychotic."[15] Such studies are no longer in fashion.

It is no longer proper to suggest that there can be as many motives for rape as there are for murder and other violent crimes. People murder for money, for love, out of jealousy, or patriotism ... the rationalizations go on and on. Rape is every bit as complex. Men rape because of sexual hunger, from a need to prove themselves, from hatred of women, or a desire for revenge, as a political statement, or from peer pressure (as in gang rapes). Men rape from a constellation of complicated motives, which become further blurred when drunkenness or drug use are part of the picture.

Perhaps the most truly political form of rape was that committed by the black activist Eldridge Cleaver, who defined his rape activity as "an insurrectionary act. It delighted me that I was defying and trampling upon the white man's law upon his system of values and that I was defiling his women.... I felt I was getting revenge."[16]

Contrast this ideology of rape with the one described in *The Crime and Consequences of Rape*: "In acquaintance rapes, the brutality and violence ... are usually absent. Since sex is the primary motivation in these cases, any classification of the motivation for rape would have to include sex in addition to power, anger, and sadism as motivating factors."[17]

Feminism needs a theory that covers both Cleaver's form of rape and that of a drunken frat brother. We need a theory that explores the complexity of the issue rather than one that oversimplifies it to fit into a political agenda.

Instead, gender feminists offer book after book of anecdotal studies that merge ideology with empirical questions. These studies make blanket and unproven assertions that have acquired the status of truth through sheer repetition. Armed with such ideological arrogance, gender feminists jettison all scientific method from their research. As the pioneering Brownmiller put it "Does one need scientific methodology in order to conclude that the anti-female propaganda that permeates our nation's cultural output promotes a climate in which acts of sexual hostility directed against women are not only tolerated but ideologically encouraged?"[18]

The answer is a clear and simple yes. One needs scientific methodology to verify any empirical claim. Without such methodology, all discussions devolve into opinion or worse. They become a barrier to real research conducted by those who are willing to reach conclusions based on data, not on opinion. Brownmiller's attitude—and that of most gender feminists—encourages bad research and false conclusions. Indeed, feminist theories of rape include such large doses of emotionally wrenching personal testimony that the validity of any statements is obscured. The statistics provided are drenched in ideology. And inconvenient facts—such as the one about 75 percent of men never raping—are ignored.

Inconvenient issues—as rape committed against men—are also ignored or sidestepped. Often the victim is considered, for all political purposes, to be a woman. This is rather like a TV interview I once watched in which Stokeley Carmichael divided the world into the white oppressor and the black oppressed. When asked about the huge global population of Orientals, he replied, "Consider them black." It is also reminiscent of another interview program, years ago, in which a Russian sociologist claimed there was no rape in Soviet Russia. When pressed on the point, the woman explained: "No word for rape exists in the Russian language, therefore there is no rape." I have no idea if her linguistic claim is true, but the methodology is familiar. By not naming a problem or by reclassifying it, the problem is made to go away.

A similar sleight of hand seems to be at work in studies on the issue of rape. Through a semantic shell game, the crime is being so redefined that it is becoming unrecognizable. The issue of date rape is a prime example of this.

Date Rape

No one can condone rape in the guise of dating. But date rape as a concept is much more than a stand against drunken frat brothers assaulting female students. Date rape has an underlying ideology. In their essay, "The Case of the Legitimate Victim," Kurt Weis and Sandra S. Borges present a sense of this underpinning:

> The dating system is a mutually exploitative arrangement of sex-role expectations which limit and direct behavior of both parties and determine the character of the relationship. Built into the concept of dating is the notion that the woman is an object which may be purchased.[19]

In other words, dating—in and of itself—is a form of exploitation and rape. In their book *The Female Fear*, Margaret T. Gordon and Stephanie Riger virtually eliminate the possibility of consent within dating: "The American dating system, which constitutes a primary source of heterosexual contacts, legitimizes the consensual 'purchase' of women as sexual objects and obliterates the crucial distinction between consent and nonconsent."[20]

By expanding the definition of rape with such wild abandon, gender feminists have blurred all clear lines on this issue. Rape used to be forced sex—a form of assault. Today, the focus has shifted from assault to so-called abuse. A recent survey by two Carleton University sociologists—financed by a $236,000 government grant—revealed that 81 percent of female students at Canadian universities and colleges had suffered sexual abuse. Their survey descended into a maelstrom of controversy when it became known that the researchers included taunts and insults during quarrels within their definition of abuse. The definition of sexual violence has been expanded to include what used to be called bad manners.

In his book, *Men Who Rape: The Psychology of the Offender*, A. Nicholas Groth provides the essential distinction between rape and sex that occurs under pressure or persuasion:

"The defining characteristic of forced assault is the risk of bodily harm to the woman should she refuse to participate in sexual activity. All nonconsenting sex is assault. In the pressured assault, the victim is sexually harassed or exploited. In forced assaults, she is a victim of rape."[21]

By eliminating the distinction between force and persuasion, important sexual lines are erased, such as the line between rape and seduction.

The New Feminist Jurisprudence

Legal lines are being erased as well. Perhaps the most important one is the presumption that a defendant is innocent until proven guilty. By requiring explicit consent in order to prove that rape has not occurred, the presumption of innocence has been reversed. The presence of force is no longer considered the defining aspect of rape; the presence of unambiguous consent is considered the defining aspect of nonrape. This makes sex itself a suspicious act.

Such policy is now law in Canada. In 1991 the Canadian government passed a "no means no" rape law, which severely narrowed the definition of consent. The definition is so broad that even if explicit consent is present, a sexual act may be deemed to be rape if the man has a position of authority over the woman.

Critics observed that such a law is patronizing to women: it assumes that they do not know their own minds or, like children or the mentally retarded, are unable to clearly communicate their desires. Such criticism does not disturb gender feminists. Catharine MacKinnon apparently sees advantages in reducing the legal status of women to that of children:

"Some of the same reasons children are granted some specific legal avenues of redress ... also hold true for the social position of women compared to men."[22]

Similar policies are spreading through courts in the United States. For example, the state of Washington held: "We believe the removal from the prior rape statute of language expressly referring to consent evidences legislative intent to shift the burden of proof on the issue to the defense."[23]

One of the time-honored legal principles that accompanies the presumption of innocence is that the prosecution must prove its case "beyond a reasonable doubt." This is part and parcel of the due process clause in the Constitution. The principle of reasonable doubt is also under attack by gender feminists. As long as the crime of rape was defined as "forced sex without consent," the burden of proving nonconsent fell to the prosecution. By altering the elements of what constitutes rape, the need for the state to argue "beyond a reasonable doubt" is removed.

No feminist wants to go back to the days when women who took rape cases to trial were emotionally shredded in the cross-examinations. None of us long for the days when the reports of a raped woman were summarily dismissed by a cynical police department and legal system. But the current attitude is as unjust to men as the former attitude was to women.

Former prosecutor Rikki Klieman complains: "Now people can be charged with virtually no evidence.... Prosecutors are not exercising very much discretion in their choice of cases. In certain places in the country, I think they're exercising none."[24]

Consent and Coercion

The pivotal difference between individualist feminists and gender feminists lies in the concepts of coercion and consent. For individualist feminists, these concepts rest on the principle of self-ownership; that is, every woman's inalienable right to control her own body. If a woman says "yes"—or if her behavior clearly implies "yes"—then consent is present. If a woman says "no"—or clearly implies it—then coercion is present. It is difficult to tell what constitutes consent or coercion for gender feminists. Consider a recent definition of sexual violence Liz Kelly offers in her book *Surviving Sexual Violence*:

> Sexual violence includes any physical, visual, verbal or sexual act that is experienced by the woman or girl, at the time or later, as a threat, invasion

or assault, that has the effect of hurting her or degrading her and/or takes away her ability to control intimate contact.[25]

In one form or another, this is becoming a common guideline for identifying sexual violence.

The first problem with this guideline is that it is totally subjective. For example, the woman need not have felt threatened during the sex act itself. As Kelly observed, "sexual violence includes any ... sexual act that is experienced by the woman or girl, at the time or *later*" as violent. In retrospect and in light of other experiences, the woman might decide that she had been coerced. But who has not regretted something in retrospect? There are many mistakes in which every one of us has been a consenting participant. Regret is not a benchmark of consent.

A second problem with the gender feminist view of rape is that it is *disastrously* subjective. It says that anything "experienced by the woman or girl" as violent is de facto violence. The coercion need not involve any physical contact: it can be simply verbal or visual. The crucial link between coercion and the use (or threat) of force has been broken. Tangible evidence of violence—such as bruises, witnesses, explicit threats, etc.—is no longer necessary for a man to be considered guilty of sexual violence. All that is necessary is for a woman to have *felt* threatened, invaded, or assaulted by him.

Any subjectivity in the definition of sexual violence has always acted against the interests of women. The issue of rape has been legally skewed in favor of the accused for so long that women have reacted by swinging the balance too far in the other direction. Gender feminists are attempting to create a virtual utopia of safety for women. Camille Paglia comments: "The point is, these white, upper-middle-class feminists believe that a pain-free world is achievable. I'm saying that a pain-free world will be achievable only under totalitarianism."[26]

Camille Paglia injects a sense of reality into the obfuscations being woven around the crucial issue of rape: "Feminism, which has waged a crusade for rape to be taken more seriously, has put young women in danger by hiding the truth about sex from them." One of the truths being hidden is that sex—by its nature—usually takes place with verbal, or even implied, consent: "In dramatizing the pervasiveness of rape, gender feminists have told young women that before they have sex with a man, they must give consent as explicit as a legal contract's. In this way, young women have been convinced that they have been the victims of rape."[27]

It is commonplace to note that the crime of rape is on the rise. Part of the perceived increase may be that more women are reporting the crime.

Ironically, several researchers suggest that women's demand for autonomy and equality may have spurred on sexual violence because men are attempting to reassert their dominance. This reaction is called backlash.

Some responsibility must be shouldered by those who tell women that they can have it all. This may be true in the best of all possible worlds, but it is not true in the inner city, on the university campus, or even in the crime-heavy suburbs. In her book, *The Trouble with Rape*, Carolyn J. Hursch notes:

> While on the one hand, through current literature women are imbued with independence, equality, and power, on the other hand, no credence is ever given to the very real fact that women are, and always will be, physically unequal to men and therefore physically vulnerable."[28]

The fact that women are vulnerable to attack means we cannot have it all. We cannot walk at night across an unlit campus or down a back alley without incurring real danger. These are things every woman *should* be able to do, but "shoulds" belong in a utopian world. They belong in a world where you drop your wallet in a crowd and have it returned, complete with credit cards and cash. A world in which unlocked Porsches are parked in the inner city. And children can be left unattended in the park. This is not the reality that confronts and confines us.

Camille Paglia introduces a bit more reality into the discussion of rape. In her book, *Sex, Art, and American Culture*, she exclaims:

> Feminism keeps ... telling women they can do anything, go anywhere, say anything, wear anything. No, they can't. Women will always be in sexual danger ... feminism, with its pie-in-the-sky fantasies about the perfect world, keeps young women from seeing life as it is."[29]

Gender feminism paints a schizophrenic picture of women. They are free and complete sexual beings, who live in a state of siege. They are empowered persons, who are terrified to open their doors at night. Their picture of men is no less confusing: even the most loving and gentle husband, father, and son is a beneficiary of the rape of women they love. No ideology that makes such vicious accusations against men as a class can heal any wounds. It can only provoke hostility in return.

For gender feminists, this antagonism may serve a purpose ... after all, gender feminism is a cry for revolution, not for reform, and revolutions are not built on conciliation. Gender feminists allow for no solution to sexual violence short of accepting their social, economic, and political agenda. They allow for no other bridge of understanding or trust to be built between men and women.

Nor does gender feminism seek to heal women on an individual basis. Even the supposedly definitive work on rape, *Against Our Will*, gives only a cursory nod to the idea of individual women healing or learning to defend themselves. Instead, individual women who have been raped are told that they will never recover from the experience ... that rape is the worst thing that can happen to a woman. Paglia observes: "The whole system now is designed to make you feel that you are maimed and mutilated forever if something like that happens. It's absolutely American—it is not European—and the whole system is filled with these clichés about sex."[30]

As a woman who has been raped, I will never downplay the trauma it brings. But being raped was not the worst thing that ever happened to me, and I have recovered from it. Feminists who say otherwise are paying me a disrespect.

The issue of rape has been diverted into a political tangle of class theory and ideology. It is time to return to the basics: consent and coercion.

Conclusion: A Call to Arms

Regarding consent the crucial question is, of course, whether a woman has agreed to have sex?, not whether she has been talked into it, bribed, manipulated, filled with regret, drunk too much, or ingested drugs. And, in an act that rarely has an explicit yes attached to it, the touchstone of consent in sex has to be the presence or absence of physical force.

On the question of force, feminists desperately need to change their focus from the man to the woman. They should be crying out for every woman to learn how to say no as effectively as possible ... and with deadly force if necessary. The true way to empower a woman and make her the equal of any man who would attack her is to teach her how to use a gun and other methods of defending herself.

There is no argument: women should be able to walk down streets alone at night and be safe. Just as they should be able to leave their apartments and car doors unlocked. Yet women who bolt their doors every night often refuse to learn self-defense because they do not believe they should have to. Because they should be able to feel safe, they refuse to take steps that would so dramatically acknowledge how unsafe they truly are.

Women have the absolute right to live without being attacked. But no right can be enjoyed for long if it is not defended, and vigorously. In June 1992 *Ladies Home Journal* ran an ad from a gun manufacturer, which read: "Self-protection is more than your right—it is your responsibility."

There is no safety for women on the streets, on the campus, or in their own homes. Violence has become so epidemic that the world seems to be going slowly crazy, and no one can rely on other people for protection. Feminism needs more women like Paxton Quigley—the author of *Armed and Female*. After a friend of hers was brutally raped, Quigley changed her perspective: she went from agitating for gun control to teaching women how to use a handgun.

Self-defense is the last frontier of feminism. And it is *the* solution— if one truly exists—to rape and other forms of violence against women. Politicizing women's pain has been a costly diversion from the hard work that is necessary to make women safe.

The fact is that rape is a crime committed against individual women, and the remedy must be an individual one as well. Women who are raped deserve one-on-one compassion and respect for the unique suffering they experience. Too much emphasis has been placed on the commonality of reactions among raped women: it is equally important to treat these women as unique human beings and respect their differences.

Equally, women who are in fear deserve one-on-one training in how to defend themselves against attack. Theories of how Neanderthal man was sexist do not offer women safety in their own homes. Rhetoric regarding patriarchy cannot protect one single woman who is dragged into the bushes. Women deserve to be empowered—not by having their pain and fear attached to a political agenda, but by learning how to use force in self-defense. Self-defense is feminism's last frontier.

Notes

1. Zsuzsanna Adler, *Rape on Trial* (London: Routledge & Kegan Paul, 1987), p. 17.

2. MacKinnon, *Feminism Unmodified*, p. 82.

3. As quoted in Mary Ann Manhart, *Rape: The First Sourcebook for Feminists*. Report from the Workshop on Self-Defense, p. 215.

4. Susan Griffin, *Rape: The Power of Consciousness* (New York: Harper & Row, 1979), p. 26.

5. Rich, *Of Woman Born*, p. 21.

6. Susan Griffin, "Rape: The All-American Crime," in *Rape Victimology*, ed. Leroy G. Schultz, Charles C. Thomas (Springfield, Ill.: Thomas, 1975), p. 3.

7. Brownmiller, *Against Our Will*, p. 8.

8. Ibid.

9. Camille Paglia, Sexual Personae: Art and Decadence from Nefertiti to Emily Dickinson (New York: Vintage Books, 1991), p. 51.

10. Brownmiller, Against Our Will, p. 14. Emphasis in the original.

11. Ibid., p. 313.

12. Andrea Parrot and Laurie Bechhofer, eds., Acquaintance Rape: The Hidden Crime, (New York: John Wiley, 1991), p. ix.

13. Brownmiller, Against Our Will, p. 391. Italics in original.

14. A. Nicholas Groth and Jean H. Birnbaum, Men who Rape: The Psychology of the Offender (New York: Plenum Press, 1979), p. 12.

15. Charles W. Dean, Mary de Bruyn-Kops, and Charles C. Thomas, eds., The Crime and Consequences of Rape (Springfield, Ill.: Thomas 1982), p. 41.

16. Eldridge Cleaver, Soul on Ice (New York: McGraw-Hill, 1967), p. 28.

17. Dean et al., Crime and Consequences of Rape, p. 44.

18. Brownmiller, Against Our Will, p. 395.

19. Kurt Weis and Sandra S. Borges, "The Case of the Legitimate Victim," in Rape Victimology, p. 112.

20. Margaret T. Gordon and Stephanie Riger, The Female Fear (New York: Free Press, 1989), p. 60.

21 Groth and Birnbaum, Men Who Rape, p. 3.

22. MacKinnon, Feminism Unmodified, p. 181.

23. State v. Camera, 113 Wash 2d. 631, 638–40, 781; Bowman, 2d, pp. 483, 487 (1989).

24. As quoted in Jack Kammer, Good Will Toward Men (New York: St. Martin's Press, 1994), p. 153.

25. Liz Kelly, Surviving Sexual Violence (Minneapolis: University of Minnesota Press, 1988), p. 41.

26. Camille Paglia, Sex, Art, and American Culture (New York: Vintage Books, 1992), p. 64.

27. Ibid., p. 49.

28. Carolyn J. Hursch, The Trouble with Rape (Chicago: Nelson-Hall, 1977), pp. 131–132.

29. Paglia, Sex, Art, and American Culture, p. 50.

30. Ibid., p. 63.

CHAPTER THREE

A Feminist Defense of Pornography

Pornography is haunting feminists, who make such bald and insupportable statements as "pornography is the theory: rape is the practice." Women who work in the porn industry, who consume pornography, or who simply disagree are all considered to be brainwashed victims of patriarchy. In other words, they are sick and need not be taken seriously. This chapter attacks the ideology and strategy behind the crusade to limit women's sexual choices. It denies that pornography degrades women.

Gender Feminists and Conservatives: An Unholy Alliance

Pornography has been a traditional battleground between conservatives, who advocate family values, and liberals, who champion freedom of expression. The political makeup of contemporary feminism is overwhelmingly liberal; the more extreme feminists—called radical or gender feminists—are socialist. Nevertheless since the mid-eighties there has been a startling sight. Feminists have been standing alongside conservatives to demand legislation against pornography. Antipornography feminists have even joined hands with fundamentalists in a common cause.

This alliance makes some feminists nervous. Lisa Duggan, Nan Hunter and Carole S. Vance, in their essay *False Promises*, summarized the amazement with which many liberal feminists view these recent events: "One is tempted to ask in astonishment, how can this be happening?... But in fact this new development is not as surprising as it at first seems. Pornography has come to be seen as a central cause of women's oppression by a significant number of feminists."[1] They also expressed great concern about the future consequences of standing side by side with conservatives: "This analysis takes feminism very close—indeed far too close to measures that will ultimately support conservative, antisex, procensorship forces in American society for it is with these forces that women have formed alliances."[2]

Gender feminists dismiss the dangers of this alliance. They discount the possibility that the legislation they seek could backlash against the feminist movement. Gender feminist Catharine MacKinnon obviated the question of whether or not to trust the law by observing: "We do not trust medicine, yet we insist it respond to women's needs. We do not trust theology, but we claim spirituality as more than a male preserve. We do not abdicate the control of technology because it was not invented by women."[3] MacKinnon concludes by dismissing those who question using patriarchy to protect women: "If women are to restrict our demands for change to spheres we can trust, spheres we already control, there will not be any."[4]

The unlikely alliance between feminists and conservatives, and the split within feminism itself, has led to strange spectacles. For example, when an antipornography ordinance was proposed in Indianapolis, the law was supported by the Moral Majority—even though it had been drafted by gender feminists. Within the local feminist community, however, the ordinance found no support. The issue of pornography is turning feminist against feminist.

The Drift Within Feminism on Pornography

The current antipornography crusade within feminism is something new on the political scene. It is new in at least two important ways: (1) it signals a break in feminism from its liberal insistence on freedom of speech and (2) it offers a revolutionary definition of pornography. The battle over pornography has shifted to new ground.

Pornography is the bête noire of gender feminism. To them, pornography is gender violence and a violation of the civil rights of women. It victimizes not merely women who work in the industry or who are exposed to magazines and films; pornography damages *all* women because it contributes to the general degradation of women that is prevalent in our society. Indeed, some theorists go so far as to claim that pornography is *the* source of society's unhealthy attitude toward women. Pornography is considered to be so damaging that it is linked, in a cause and effect relationship, to violent crimes such as rape. Thus, eliminating this form of expression is viewed as self-defense, not censorship.

The legal theorist Catharine MacKinnon has been a key voice in the antipornography campaign. In her book *Feminism Unmodified*, MacKinnon defined the object of attack: "Pornography, in the feminist view, is a form of forced sex, a practice of sexual politics, an institution of gender inequality."[5] MacKinnon claims that pornography is not just a form of expression; pornographic material is—in and of itself—an act of violence: "Pornography not only teaches the reality of male dominance. It is one way its reality is imposed as well as experienced. It is a way of seeing and treating women."[6]

MacKinnon further erases the line between attitude and behavior, image and action:

> Male power makes authoritative a way of seeing and treating women, so that when a man looks at a pornographic picture—pornographic meaning that the woman is defined as to be acted upon, a sexual object, a sexual thing—the *viewing* is an *act*, an act of male supremacy. [Emphasis in the original.][7]

The wholesale condemnation of pornography is new in feminism. Since its revival in the early 1960s the movement has been dominated by socialists and liberals; both these traditions advocated freedom of speech. Moreover, pornography tended to be viewed as part of a larger trend toward sexual liberation—a liberation that feminists applauded because it ushered in such things as birth control and the unveiling of women's sexuality.

Lisa Duggan, Nan Hunter, and Carole S. Vance typified this attitude in acknowledging the possible benefits pornography offered to women. They note that pornography has "served to flout conventional sexual mores, to ridicule sexual hypocrisy and to underscore the importance of sexual needs." In short, pornography has liberated women from the status quo by transmitting many messages:

> It advocates sexual adventure, sex outside of marriage, sex for pleasure, casual sex, illegal sex, anonymous sex, public sex, voyeuristic sex. Some of these ideas appeal to women ... who may interpret some images as legitimating their own sense of sexual urgency or desire to be sexually aggressive."[8]

Pornography and feminism have much in common. Both deal with women as sexual beings and both attempt to bring this sexuality out into the open. Moreover, pornography and feminism share a history of being targeted by obscenity laws. In particular, the Comstock Laws of the 1870s were used not only against pornographic material but also against birth control information. Feminist material—especially lesbian material—has always suffered under laws regulating sexual expression.

Gender Feminists: The New Puritans

By the late 1970s sexual liberation was being viewed with suspicion by feminists. Pornography was being redefined as an enemy of women. In her book, *Our Blood*, gender feminist Andrea Dworkin spells this out: "In pornography, sadism is the means by which men establish their dominance. Sadism is the authentic exercise of power which confirms manhood; and the first characteristic of manhood is that its existence is based on the negation of the female."[9] Dworkin explains that manhood requires the destruction of women's bodies and will. Why? Dworkin explains this as well:

> The sexual sadism actualizes male identity.... The common erotic project of destroying women makes it possible for men to unite into a brotherhood; this project is the only firm and trustworthy groundwork for cooperation among males and all male bonding is based on it."[10]

Antiporn Strategy

The feminist attack on pornography is not merely another cry for censorship from those who hate sex. It is more sophisticated than that. Feminists are using a strategy that has proved successful with other issues, such as affirmative action. Pornography is being defined as a violation of women's civil rights. Thus, instead of advocating criminal proceedings against pornographers, feminists restrict themselves to civil suits. This approach avoids sticky constitutional questions; in particular, it avoids the First Amendment. It also turns the entire discussion of pornography on its head. Conventional arguments for and against pornography simply do not apply.

Traditional obscenity laws have focused on the connection between pornography and moral harm. One of the standard tests of obscenity came from Supreme Court Justice Brennan in his ruling on *Memoirs v. Massachusetts*:

> (a) The dominant theme of the material taken as a whole appeals to the prurient interest in sex; (b) the material is patently offensive because it

affronts contemporary community standards relating to the description or representation of sexual matters; and (c) the material is utterly without redeeming social value."

Antipornography feminists dwell on the connection between pornography and political harm—namely, the oppression of women. Consider MacKinnon's presentation of how pornography differs from obscenity. She argues that obscenity is concerned with morality—white male morality. Pornography is concerned with politics—the politics of women's subjugation. She further distinguishes between the two: "Morality here means good and evil; politics means power and powerlessness. Obscenity is a moral idea; pornography is a political practice. Obscenity is abstract; pornography is concrete. The two concepts represent two entirely different things."[11]

In the mid-eighties, gender feminists launched a campaign to pass antipornography ordinances on a city by city basis. By localizing the issue, they bypassed the problem of obtaining a national consensus, which had proven so difficult with the ERA. The first ordinance—drafted by MacKinnon and Dworkin—served as the model for future ones. This was the Minneapolis Ordinance of 1983. In addressing the Minneapolis City Council, MacKinnon declared the key theme of gender feminism's attack on pornography: namely, that pornography was a violation of civil rights— an act of discrimination against women:

> We are proposing ... a statutory scheme that will situate pornography as a central practice in the subordination of women.... The understanding and the evidence which we will present to you today to support defining pornography as a practice of discrimination on the basis of sex is a new idea.[12]

Further, pornography was now placed at the heart of how men oppress women: "Pornography conditions and determines the way in which men actually treat women ... and we will show that it is central to the way in which women remain second-class citizens."[13]

Under the ordinance's provisions, a woman who had worked in pornography—a *Playboy* centerfold, for example—could bring a civil lawsuit against her employers for having coerced her into a "pornographic performance." Laws and remedies already existed for fraud or for contracts signed under duress. The purpose of the ordinance was to make "coercion" into a civil matter.

The definition of coercion was all-important. The ordinance was clear. Coercion was deemed to be present even if the woman was of age, fully understood the nature of the performance, signed a contract and release, agreed to it before witnesses, was under no threat, and was fully paid. None of these factors provided evidence of consent.

In essence, consent was not possible. In principle, the woman could not be treated as a consenting adult. By definition, coercion was always present in a pornographic act.

MacKinnon later explained: "In the context of unequal power (between the sexes), one needs to think about the meaning of consent—whether it is a meaningful concept at all."[14] Gloria Steinem, in her introduction to Linda Lovelace's exposé *Out of Bondage*, agreed: "The question is free will: Are the subjects of pornography there by choice, or by coercion, *economic* or physical."(Emphasis added.)[15]

In other words, if the woman needed or wanted the money offered, this would constitute economic coercion. The politics of society made it impossible for women to fully consent to a pornographic act. Women who thought they had agreed were mistaken. Such women had been so damaged by a male dominated culture that they were not able to give true consent. Lisa Duggan, Nan Hunter, and Carole S. Vance observe: "Advocates of the ordinance effectively assume that women have been so conditioned by the pornographic world view that if their own experiences of the sexual acts ... are not subordinating, then they must simply be victims of false consciousness."[16]

My Background as a Defender of Pornography

Several years ago, antipornography feminists attempted to pass an ordinance in Los Angeles. I was among the feminists who went down to city hall to argue against the ordinance. The arguments I decided *not* to use are almost as revealing as the ones I settled on.

I decided not to argue that pornography is undefinable and, therefore, not appropriate for a legal system that requires a clear point of enforcement. The ordinance had defined what it meant by pornography in excruciating—if subjective—detail. To focus on definitions would be to divert the debate into the bogs of what constitutes "dehumanization" or "exploitation." I simply accepted the rule of thumb offered by Supreme Court Justice Potter Stewart in his ruling on *Jacobellis v. Ohio*, 1964: "I know it when I see it." I assumed that everyone was talking about the same thing.

I also abandoned appeals to the First Amendment. Antipornography feminists had a tangled web of counterarguments, which would require more time to answer than I would be allotted. MacKinnon's arguments are typical. She begins by attacking the Constitution as a "white male" document: "The First Amendment essentially presumes some level of social equality among people and hence essentially equal social access to the means of expression. In a context of inequality between the sexes, we cannot presume that that is accurate."[17]

MacKinnon then adds the dual claims: freedom of speech is not necessary for human fulfillment and pornography is an act of violence, not a form of speech: "The First Amendment also presumes that for the mind to be free to fulfill itself, speech must be free and open…. Pornography amounts to terrorism and promotes not freedom but silence. Rather, it promotes freedom for men and enslavement and silence for women."[18] If pornography was an act of violence, then the First Amendment was irrelevant.

I also avoided a discussion of privacy rights. Supreme Court Justice Thurgood Marshall (*Stanley v. Georgia*, 1969) had maintained: "If the First Amendment means anything, it means that a state has no business telling a man, sitting alone in his own house, what books he may read or what films he must watch." But, again, if pornography was violence, the issue of committing it in private was beside the point.

The only way to effectively challenge the new attack was to answer gender feminists in their own terms. The debate on pornography had been shifted to new ground. Thus, the key questions were: Are all women coerced into pornography? and How does pornography relate to violence against women? Everything seemed to return to the basic contention of feminists: pornography is an act of violence. It is an act committed upon and against unconsenting women. This is the level on which the assault on pornography must be addressed.

A Feminist Defense of Pornography

To begin with, I divided women into two categories: women who were directly involved with pornography—either in production or consumption and women who had no direct exposure. The first category is the litmus test. If women are degraded by pornography, surely the women closest to it would be the most deeply affected. At the heart of this question is the problem of pinning down subjective terms such as "degrading."

It was not possible to ask every woman who was involved in pornography whether or not she felt degraded by it. This left only one way to judge the matter. Namely, did women freely chose to work in the porn industry or to consume pornography?

The answer is clear: pornographic models and actresses sign contracts. Women who produce pornography, such as Ms. Hefner at *Playboy* or Candida Royalle at Femme Films do so willingly.[19] Women shopkeepers who stock pornography chose to fill in the order forms. Women who consume pornography—including me—pay money to do so.

However, gender feminists insist, no "healthy" woman would consent to the humiliation of pornography. Therefore, women who make this choice are so psychologically damaged by a male dominated culture that they are incapable of true consent. In Indianapolis, the ordinance explicitly argued that women, like children, need special protection under the law.

Pause with me for a moment. Consider how insulting this is to women who have made an "unacceptable" choice with their bodies—that is, women who work in pornography. Antipornography feminists label these women as psychologically sick because they have made nonfeminist choices. These women are called victims of their culture.

But gender feminists were raised in the same culture. Presumably, these "enlightened" women wish us to believe that their choices are based on reason and knowledge; somehow, they have risen above the culture in which they were raised. They are unwilling, however, to grant such a courteous assumption to any woman who disagrees with them.

Gender feminists are adamant that women involved in the production of pornography cannot be held legally responsible for their actions because they are psychologically impaired by cultural influence. Their arguments need not be taken seriously, their contracts need not be respected. They are psychologically impaired. If a woman enjoys consuming pornography, it is not because she comes from another background, has a different emotional makeup, or has reasoned from different facts. No, it is because she is mentally incompetent. Like any three-year-old, she is unable to give informed consent regarding her own body.

The touchstone principle of feminism used to be, "a woman's body, a woman's right." Regarding date rape, feminists still declare, "No means no." The logical corollary of this is, "Yes means yes." Now, modern feminists are declaring that "yes" means nothing. It is difficult to believe that any form of pornography could be more degrading to women than this attitude.

As to whether cultural pressure has influenced women's decisions—of course it has. The culture we live in impacts on every choice we make. But to say that women who participate in pornography cannot make a choice because of cultural pressure, is to eliminate the possibility of choice in any realm. Because every choice of every person is made in the presence of cultural pressure—including the choice to become a feminist.

The Right to Pose is the Right to Contract

The antipornography ordinances were intended to protect women from the consequences of their own actions. But what legal implications does this have for women's contracts—a right for which past generations fought hard? In the nineteenth century, women battled to become the legal equal of men, to have their consent taken seriously in the form of contracts, and to have control of their own bodies legally recognized. After the antipornography crusade, who will take a woman's consent seriously? When the Fifteenth Amendment was proposed in a form that enfranchised black men while ignoring women, the pioneering feminist Susan B. Anthony protested: "We have stood with the black man in the Constitution over a half a century.... Enfranchise him and we are left outside with lunatics, idiots and criminals."[20]

To deprive women of the right to make their own contracts is to place them, once again, outside the constitution with lunatics, idiots, and criminals. Gender feminists are reducing a woman's consent to a legal triviality. Women are being granted the protection of no longer being taken seriously when they sign contracts. This is not a step toward dignity or freedom for women.

But what of the women who do not chose to be involved in pornography? What of the women who are offended by it? The simplistic answer is that they should not buy or consume it. Moreover, they should use any and all peaceful means to persuade others that pornography is not a proper form of expression.

The Bias of Researchers

The argument runs that whether or not women are directly exposed to pornography, they are still victimized. Pornography is the first step of a slippery slope that leads to explicit violence against women, such as rape. Thus, *every* woman is a victim, because every woman is in danger. This argument assumes: (1) that pornography impacts on men's behavior, (2) that the impact can be measured objectively, and (3) that it can be correlated with sexual violence.

Pornography probably does impact on people's behavior, but it is next to impossible to objectively measure that impact. Human psychology is extremely complex, especially in the area of sexual response. Moreover, the standard of measurement and the conclusions drawn from data usually depend on the bias of the researchers or of those who commission the research.

For example, in 1983 the Metropolitan Toronto Task Force on Violence Against Women commissioned Thelma McCormack to study pornography's connection with sexual aggression. Her research did not support the assumption that there was one. Indeed, McCormack's study indicated that the effect of pornography might be cathartic. It might reduce the incidence of rape.

Her report, *Making Sense of Research on Pornography*, was discarded.[21] The study was reassigned to David Scott, a nonfeminist committed to antipornography. Scott found a clear connection between pornography and sexual aggression. Students, journalists, and researchers who tried to obtain a copy of McCormack's paper were told that it was unavailable.

Statistics almost always contain assumptions and biases. Sometimes the bias is obvious and acknowledged. For example, a researcher who believes that sexual aggression is a learned behavior will naturally ask different questions than someone who believes aggression is an instinct. Other forms of bias are not so obvious.

However, for the sake of argument, let's assume that a correlation exists between pornography and rape. What would such a correlation prove? If a society with more pornography tended to have more rape, what would this say? A correlation is not a cause and effect relationship. It is a logical fallacy to assume that if A is correlated with B, then A causes B. Both might be caused by a totally separate factor, C. For example, there is a high correlation between the number of doctors in a city and the amount of alcohol consumed there. One does not cause the other. Both result from a third factor, the size of the city's population.

Similarly, a correlation between pornography and rape may indicate nothing more than a common cause for both, namely, that we live in a sexually repressed society. To further repress sex by restricting pornography might well increase the incidence of rape. Opening up the area of pornography might well diffuse sexual violence by making it more understandable.

Conclusion

There is great irony in the spectacle of gender feminists aligning themselves with their two greatest ideological enemies: conservatives and the patriarchal state. In using ordinances, antipornography feminists are legitimizing a system they themselves condemn as patriarchy. It is a strange leap of faith. After all, once a law is on the books, it is the state bureaucracy, not NOW, who will enforce it. In *Our Blood*, Andrea Dworkin excoriated patriarchal bureaucracy:

Under patriarchy, no woman is safe to live her life, or to love, or to mother children. Under patriarchy, every woman is a victim, past, present, and future. Under patriarchy, every woman's daughter is a victim, past, present, and future. Under patriarchy, every woman's son is her potential betrayer and also the inevitable rapist or exploiter of another woman.[22]

Now feminists are appealing to this same state as a protector.

The final irony is that it is the state—not free speech—that has been the oppressor of women. It was the state, not pornography, that burned women as witches. It was eighteenth-century law, not pornography, that defined women as chattel. Nineteenth-century laws allowed men to commit wayward women to insane asylums, to claim their wives' earnings, and to beat them with impunity. Twentieth-century laws refuse to recognize rape within marriage and sentence the sexes differently for the same crime. The state, not pornography, has raised barriers against women. And censorship, not freedom, will keep the walls intact.

One of the most important questions confronting feminism at the turn of this century is whether or not women's liberation can embrace sexual liberation. Can the freedom of women and freedom of speech become fellow travelers once more?

The feminist Myrna Kostash answered this question well: "To paraphrase Albert Camus, freedom to publish and read does not necessarily assure a society of justice and peace, but without these freedoms it has no assurance at all."[23]

Notes

1. Lisa Duggan, Nan Hunter, and Carole S. Vance, "False Promises: Feminist Antipornography Legislation in the U.S.," in *Women Against Censorship*, ed. Varda Burstyn (Toronto: Douglas & McIntyre, 1985), p. 131.
2. Ibid.
3. MacKinnon, *Feminism Unmodified*, p. 228.
4. Ibid.
5. Ibid., p. 148.
6. Ibid., p. 130.
7. Ibid.
8. Duggan et al., "False Promises," p. 145.
9. Dworkin, *Our Blood*, p. 16.
10. Ibid.
11. MacKinnon, *Feminism Unmodified*, p. 147.
12. As quoted in *Pornography and Challenge to Free Speech and Obscenity*, p. xii.
13. Ibid.
14. Catharine MacKinnon as quoted in *Toronto Star*, February 17, 1992.
15. Gloria Steinem, "Introduction," in Linda Lovelace, *Out of Bondage* (Secaucus, N.J.: Lyle Stuart, 1986), p. 9.

16. Duggan et al., "False Promises," p. 143.

17. MacKinnon, *Feminism Unmodified*, p. 129–130.

18. Ibid.

19. See Wendy McElroy *XXX: A Woman's Right to Pornography* (New York: St. Martin's Press, 1995), pp. 146–191 for interviews with women in pornography, all of whom maintain that their involvement is voluntary and rewarding.

20. Quoted in William L. O'Neill, *Everyone Was Brave: A History of Feminism in America* (New York: Quadrant Press, 1971), p. 17.

21. One of the few places this report is available is through a reprint in *Women Against Censorship*.

22. Dworkin, as quoted in *Liberty*, p. 58.

23. Myrna Kostash, "Second Thoughts," in *Women Against Censorship*, p. 37.

CHAPTER FOUR

Sexual Harassment

Many men have derogatory attitudes toward women and express them in inappropriate ways. The question is whether the government should control sexual attitudes. In the touchy issue of sexual harassment, gender feminists have found a weapon with which they can regulate the marketplace. The casualties are freedom of speech, the free market, and the right of every human being to hold sexually incorrect attitudes.

Historical Background

In 1886 the individualist-feminist Gertrude Kelly described the soul-deadening effect men's sexual attitudes can have on women:

> Men, for some purpose of their own, which they probably best understand, have always denied to women the opportunity to think; and, if some women have had courage enough to dare public opinion, and insist on thinking for themselves, they have been so beaten by that most powerful weapon in society's arsenal, ridicule, that it has effectually prevented the great majority from making any attempt to come out of slavery.[1]

Over a century later the 1990s are confronting the issue of sexual harassment head-on, especially as it occurs in the workplace. Men feel misunderstood, women feel outraged. Courts are puzzling over this ill-defined crime, which often seems to have no objective standards of evidence. Meanwhile, businesses scramble to formulate sexual harassment policies that will help to insulate them from legal liability.

The issue of sexual harassment has been brought to the forefront of controversy by gender feminists, who view it as yet another way patriarchy maintains its dominance over women. They consider it to be a gender crime—a crime that men commit against women.

With all the controversy and liability that adheres to the issue of sexual harassment, one question becomes crucial: What is it? One of the problems in defining sexual harassment is that it is usually discussed in emotional terms or legalistic ones. It is time to step back from the rhetoric and accusations surrounding this issue and examine it objectively.

Harassment as a Legal Issue

As a legal and political issue, sexual harassment has its roots in Title VII, the fair employment provision of the Civil Rights Act of 1964. Section 703(a) of Title VII states:

> It shall be an unlawful employment practice for an employer to fail or refuse to hire or to discharge any individual or otherwise to discriminate against an individual with respect to his compensation, terms, conditions or privileges of employment, because of such individual's race, color, religion, sex, or national origin.

Title VII was designed to outlaw racial discrimination in the workplace. It has been extended to cover sexual harassment, which is viewed as sexual or gender discrimination.

On July 2, 1965—the same day the Civil Rights Act of 1964 became law—the Equal Employment Opportunity Commission opened its doors as an agency to enforce the private right to nondiscrimination in employment. On that date, the *New York Times* published job listings, which were segregated according to "male" and "female." A box heading the section explained that, in compliance with the Civil Rights Act, the *Times* urged qualified job-seekers to reply to both listings.

Despite this sensitivity, *Barnes v. Train*—the first sexual harassment case to reach the courts—was not litigated until 1974, almost ten years after passage of the Civil Rights Act. In this case, the plaintiff claimed she lost her position for refusing to have sex with her boss. The court found that such a situation was not addressed by the Civil Rights Act.

The following year, in *Corne v. Bausch and Lomb, Inc.*, two female employees claimed "involuntary resignations": that is, they claimed their supervisor's physical and verbal harassment forced them to resign. The Arizona Federal District Court said it would be ludicrous to hold that the sort of activity involved in this case was contemplated by the Civil Rights Act. Until 1981 sexual harassment was a term that was rarely heard.

In 1981, however, *Bundy v. Jackson* argued that sexual harassment was a violation of Title VII—even if the victim had incurred no tangible loss.

The legal establishment came to accept sexual harassment as being actionable under Title VII. The Equal Employment Opportunity Commission (EEOC) began to pursue cases on behalf of plaintiffs and to protect them from retaliatory action. The 1980 EEOC guidelines defined sexual harassment with the following statement:

> Harassment on the basis of sex is a violation of Section 703 of Title VII. Unwelcome sexual advances, requests for sexual favors, and other verbal or physical conduct of a sexual nature constitute sexual harassment when: (1) submission to such conduct is made either explicitly or implicitly a term or condition of an individual's employment; (2) submission to or rejections of such conduct by an individual is used as the basis for employment decisions affecting such individual; or (3) such conduct has the purpose or effect of unreasonably interfering with an individual's work performance or creating an intimidating, hostile, or offensive environment.

In 1984 the EEOC amended its sexual harassment guidelines as follows:

> An employer is responsible for the acts and those of its agents and supervisory employees with respect to sexual harassment regardless of whether the specific acts complained of were authorized or even forbidden by the employer and regardless of whether the employer knew or should have known of the occurrence.

This amendment placed all burden of blame squarely at the feet of the employer, who is responsible (and liable) for any act of sexual harassment within his or her business.

In 1986 the U.S. Supreme Court handed down a landmark decision on *Meritor Savings Bank v. Vinson.* Here, the plaintiff Vinson alleged that she had agreed to sex with her boss out of fear of losing her job. A district court had ruled that she was a willing participant. This was reversed on appeal. The U.S. Supreme Court found that the nub of the issue was not whether the sex act was voluntary but whether it was welcomed.

Under the new Civil Rights Act of 1991, victims of sexual harassment can be awarded limited compensatory and punitive damages if they prove they were intentionally discriminated against. Previously, the courts could award only lost pay, benefits, and some legal expenses.

As the debate about sexual harassment heats up, one question becomes crucial: What *is* it?

Toward a Definition

Perhaps the most frequently asked question about sexual harassment is: What is it? Which specific behaviors constitute sexual harassment? The term seems to cover everything from rudeness to rape.

The legal system has evolved an answer. In general, sexual harassment has been divided into two categories: (1) a quid pro quo, by which sexual favors are directly traded for professional gain; and (2) a hostile working environment, in which women are threatened and disempowered. In 1980 the EEOC found that sexual harassment included physical, verbal, and environmental abuse.

It is the subtle form of sexual harassment—"a hostile working environment"—that has caused the most confusion. What is a "hostile working environment"? Does it include jokes, compliments, graffiti, cartoons? The term "a hostile working environment" was coined in the 1970s by the gender feminist and legal theorist, Catharine MacKinnon, who did not provide a clear definition. Indeed, when courts have to assess whether an environment is hostile, they often invoke a reasonable person standard. This means, they ask whether the workplace includes behavior that a reasonable person would find threatening. A hostile work environment has been found to include jokes or unsolicited compliments. Indeed, it is any verbal conduct that makes the recipient feel uncomfortable or humiliated.

In essence, free speech is offered less protection in the workplace than at home or on the streets. Why? Because offensive sexual remarks—even very subtle ones—are considered to be a form of hate speech. Feminist Susan Faludi comments on why men inflict such humiliation on women: "It's more the subtler form of making women uncomfortable by turning the workplace into a locker room and then telling them, 'What's the matter, you can't handle it? You wanted equality; I'm going to give it to you with a vengeance.'"[2]

Seeking Definition with Academia

Historically, universities have been bastions of intellectual liberty, where freedom of speech has been accepted as a precondition for knowledge. Ironically, they are becoming centers of censorship, where unacceptable views of women are being silenced. Universities have rushed to formulate policies and to define sexual harassment. One of the most commonly cited definitions comes from the researcher F. J. Tilly, who deemed sexual harassment in academia to be "the use of authority to emphasize the sexuality or sexual identity of a student in a manner which prevents or impairs the student's full enjoyment of educational benefits, climate, or opportunities."[3]

Tilly identified five types of sexual harassment, including general sexual comments; inappropriate sexual advances, which occur without sanction; sexual advances, which have the promise of rewards; sexual advances, which hold the threat of punishment; and sexual assaults. Gender feminists take this definition one step farther. According to Nancy Tuana even innocent social meetings can occur within a coercive context; e.g., the power differential between a professor and student enables this. An act can be coercive even if the person in power does not intend it to be so. This is what Tuana calls an "implicit unintended threat [with] no intention to harm."[4]

Universities across the nation have scrambled to conform with this new form of political correctness, which might be called sexual correctness. For example, in September 1989 Harvard University issued a guideline that removed any connection between behavior and intent. In other words, sexual harassment can occur even though the transgressor was a man of goodwill, with absolutely no intention of harm. In the section, "Sexism in the Classroom," the Harvard guideline cautioned against innocent remarks that might be taken the wrong way. Such remarks constituted harassment: "Alienating messages may be subtle and even unintentional, but they nevertheless tend to compromise the learning experience of both sexes.... For example ... calling only upon women in a class on topics such as marriage and the family."

In a recent book entitled *Who Stole Feminism?: How Women Have Betrayed Women*, Christina Hoff Sommers detailed the disastrous effects such policies can have on academic freedom.[5] At a university in Minnesota, four female students accused all the tenured staff of the Scandinavian studies department (five men and one woman) of sexual harassment. The students filed formal charges, accusing the staff of, among other things, allegedly harassing the students by not giving them higher grades; one professor was said to have greeted a student in an unfriendly manner; another supposedly gave a "patriarchal" interpretation of Isak Dinesen's work; one did not read a novel the student had recommended.

Among the students' demands for a remedy were: the denial of merit pay for not less than five years and monthly sexual harassment workshops for at least twelve months. No one at the university stood up for the accused professors. Finally, all charges were dropped, without explanation.

Outside of academia, the Ninth U.S. Circuit Court complicated the issue even more in a landmark decision. Judge Robert Beezer ruled that women are protected from any remark or behavior that a "reasonable woman" would have problems with. The court also introduced a double standard into the law by declaring that some behavior acceptable to men may be legally actionable by women. This ruling reflected the general belief that no situation comparable to sexual harassment exists for men.

No wonder men are becoming resentful. They are being backed into a corner by accusations that seem to have no rules of evidence and little burden of proof. Men's compassion has been replaced by exasperated demands for a specific list of things they are no longer allowed to say or do, for a clear definition of what constitutes sexual harassment. A definition that does not include vague, subjective terms like "discomfort." This is a fair request.

Sexual harassment cannot be objectively defined without defining what constitutes offensive behavior. What offends people varies widely, depending on their upbringing and their attitudes. For example, calling a woman "honey" in the South is a harmless verbal convention. Because of these factors, sexual harassment is a subjective term that depends on the personalities and cultural backgrounds of the people involved.

This subjectivity is reflected not merely in vague definitions, but in the lack of consensus on what is sexually offensive. If a woman welcomes her boss's advances, is this sexual harassment or romance? Is it career advancement? When is it inappropriate to comment on a woman's appearance? What if she has just lost twenty pounds through strenuous effort? Is it rude to ignore her success or harassment to commend it? Moral theorists like Kenneth Cooper argue that "regardless of how harmless these appreciative comments may seem, they are put-downs which lower the group stature of the target."[6]

Even among feminists, the term sexual harassment is defined in markedly differently ways. Consider the opinion of feminist Ellen Frankel Paul, a professor at Bowling Green State University, who makes a key distinction:

> Outrageous acts—sexual harassment per se—must be legally redressable. Lesser but not trivial offenses ... should be considered moral lapses for which the offending party receives opprobrium, disciplinary warnings, or penalties, depending on the setting and the severity.[7]

Yet many other feminists consider even the act of looking at a woman in an unacceptable manner—ogling or leering—to constitute sexual harassment.

Competing Models of Sexual Harassment

Accompanying this lack of definition—or, perhaps, contributing to it—are two different and mutually exclusive models of sexual harassment.

The first model contends that sexual comments and behavior within the workplace—and within bounds—are the natural result of the general biological attraction between men and women. Mutual attraction is as natural in the workplace as it is anywhere else. Real sexual harassment, where women have to fend off persistent and unwanted advances, comes from a small minority of men, just as domestic violence against women comes from small minority of husbands. According to the natural attraction model, there is no systematic pattern of sexual harassment within the workplace. It is an individual and unfortunate act, which companies should remedy privately through proper employment policies. This interpretation is usually dismissed as trivializing sexual harassment. Those who espouse it are vigorously accused of insensitivity to women.

The second model views sexual harassment as the natural result of how the institutions of society, such as universities or the free market, are structured. These institutions are an expression of patriarchy: the political system by which men, particularly white males, oppress women. Sexual harassment is an inevitable and pervasive aspect of patriarchy. This is the dominant feminist position and the one most commonly heard in the media.

According to this model, sexual harassment cannot be privately remedied. The government—which feminists usually decry as oppressive to women—should intervene in the workplace to protect women. Remedies cannot be private or individual, because the so-called crime itself is not direct against any particular woman so much as it is against women as a class. MacKinnon admonishes us that "sexual harassment ... is a group-defined injury which occurs to many different individuals, among all of which a single characteristic—female sex—is shared. Such an injury is *in essence* a group injury." (Emphasis in the original.)[8]

With no clear definition and with models that so directly contradict each other, it is no wonder that many, if not most, of the studies on sexual harassment have produced little data of value.

The Inadequacy of Studies

Since the late 1970s a flood of studies has examined sexual harassment, particularly in the workplace and on campuses. Most of them are flawed on

several levels. One of these inadequacies is a lack of a common methodology. This—along with no common definition of sexual harassment—
has led to many problems. For example, it is next to impossible to compare studies that use incompatible data or standards.

Moreover, in many of the studies, the sampling (the number of
respondents) is either too small or not random enough to give a true
reading on the prevalence and nature of sexual harassment. For example,
F. J. Tilly's widely reported survey suffers from an extremely limited
response rate. Of 8,000 surveys distributed only 259 were returned.[9]

Furthermore, most of the studies on sexual harassment have focused
on large public institutions, such as universities, and government agencies. One of the most frequently cited and influential studies was conducted by the U.S. Merit Systems Protection Board in 1981. In survey-
ing over 20,000 women, the study found that 42 percent of the women
had experienced sexual harassment within the prior twenty-four months.
Their 1988 follow-up study rendered the same results. But the sampling
was only from federal government employees and the definition of sexual harassment was "unwanted sexual attention."[10]

The conclusions from studies of public agencies are almost always
extended to the free market. Often, they are extended in the form of
regulations. But free-market institutions function quite differently from
public ones. Merely one of these differences is that businesses need to be
fiercely competitive to survive. Their chances of survival often hinges on
hiring and keeping the best employees. A company that abuses women
will lose valuable employees, who will go on to enrich its competition.
A company that tolerates sexual harassment will become less profitable.
The same cannot be said of government agencies, which do not need to
obey the marketplace to survive.

Bias also plays a large role in the studies of sexual harassment. There
are several reasons for this. One is that many of the studies are conducted by those with an ideological bent, namely, that of gender feminism. Another source of bias is the media's natural tendency toward sen-
sationalism. For example, the September 1992 issue of *Seventeen* ran a
questionnaire on sexual harassment, which was preceded by an emotion-
laden story of a woman's ordeal in the face of harassment. The questionnaire was designed by Dr. Nan Stein of the Wellesley College Center for Research on Women. One of her questions was whether anyone
had *forced* any of the following behaviors upon the student in the last
school year: any sexual contact, such as a touch, pinch, or grab; any lean-
ing over or "cornering"; any sexual notes or pictures; suggestive gestures,
looks, or jokes; pressure to engage in any sexual act.

In *Who Stole Feminism*, Christina Hoff Sommers observed that only 0.2 percent of readers responded and based this estimate on the number of subscribers. The readers who took the time to respond were almost certainly the ones who felt most strongly about the subject. Sommers comments: "What Ms. Stein ... had devised is known as a self-selecting poll. Responsible pollsters call them SLOPs—self-selected listener opinion polls—and they avoid doing them, or crediting them when other pollsters do them."[11]

A potent source of bias regarding sexual harassment comes from the fact that so much of the research is done by those whose livelihood depends on its existence. In 1988 the magazine *Working Woman* reported that "sexual harassment costs a typical Fortune 500 service or manufacturing company $6.7 million a year."[12] Most of this expenditure goes to consultants, seminars, and training programs. Consulting on sexual harassment is one of America's growth industries. The industry was formed when the Supreme Court found in case of the *Meritor Savings Bank v. Vinson* that companies could limit their liability to harassment claims by implementing antiharassment policies. It can be easily argued, that such consultants have a vested interest in revealing sexual harassment as a problem that needs remedy.

Until there are unbiased researchers who randomly select samples of females and males, there can be no truly useful studies. Until studies are conducted with the same methodology and definitions, their data cannot be compared. Respondent rates need to be higher. Findings need to be reported in their entirety. Policy and law should not be based on the flawed and inconsistent studies available today.

What Is the Purpose of Law?

The purpose of the EEOC is to regulate social behavior to protect citizens against harm from the private or public sectors. In short, the EEOC aims at social regulation. More and more, this is a function government is assuming. Between 1900 and 1964 only one such regulatory agency was established. Between 1964 and 1972 seven agencies were created, including the EEOC.[13] These agencies tend toward rule-making rather than "cease-and-desist" actions. That is, they aim at promoting positive actions rather than merely at preventing negative ones.

An important question is therefore whether the government should mandate social attitudes, including sexual ones. Should a government control and punish the bad attitudes of its citizens? What is the proper purpose of laws in society? In the classical liberal tradition the purpose of laws is to protect the rights—that is, the person and property—of individuals. In other words, the law should prohibit and punish acts of violence. It should not concern itself with peaceful attitudes or nonviolent actions.

Contrast this with the view of law implicit in attempts to legislate sexual harassment. Feminists are using the law not to protect rights, but to enforce a proper standard of morality—a standard that demands a certain type and level of respect for women. A driving force behind these laws is socialist or gender feminism. In turn, this form of feminism is a building block of political correctness—the movement that considers virtually all of Western culture to be racist and sexist. Those who are politically correct seek to correct this injustice by championing the victims of Western civilization.

The legal system is being used to enforce their ideal of virtue. From this perspective, certain so-called bad attitudes, comments, and behavior ought to be prohibited, whether or not they are peaceful. Because men should not hold or express opinions that are degrading to women, the law punishes men who err. The correct moral position becomes mandated by law.

Perhaps the most fundamental human freedom is the right to weigh evidence and to reach a conclusion. This means people have a right to reach conclusions that are wrong and offensive. If men can be taken to court because they express the wrong attitude toward women, this says that women have the right to tell men which opinions they are legally allowed to hold. More than this—it says that the government has a right to regulate opinions.

Freedom of speech is a liberty to which the weakest members of society (such as women) should cling. After all, if moral and cultural standards can be imposed by law, it will not be the weak who decide which standard is enforced. Offensive speech is far less dangerous to women than censorship.

The Creation of Conflict

The current policies of the EEOC create a number of serious moral/political issues, including the following:

   1. *The Breaching of Free Speech.* An individual's right to hold and to express socially unacceptable beliefs is being denied through laws against sexual speech in the workplace. More and more, the law prohibits and punishes politically incorrect views of women.

   2. *Government Intrusion into Privacy.* By regulating nonviolent sexual

behavior, the government has crossed over a line that has traditionally separated the personal from the political. Traditionally, nonviolent sexual behavior has been a privacy issue.

3. Erosion of the Free Market. In regulating behavior in the workplace, the government has extended its authority over the marketplace. It has further erased the distinction between the private and the public sectors.

4. Government as a Father Figure. Ironically, feminists are turning to the government they condemn as oppressive and ask for its protection. They are moving from patriarchy to paternalism.

One of the largest problems created by sexual harassment laws, however, is rarely discussed, namely, their social cost.

The Social Cost of Sexual Harassment Laws

It is estimated that 75 percent of American companies have instituted sexual harassment policies. These businesses spend huge amounts of money to educate employees on this issue. But money is only one of the costs of sexual harassment.

Among the less visible costs are:

1. Women are being returned to the status of victims. In the 1960s and '70s, feminism told women to stand firmly on their own two feet, to demand respect, and to give as good as they got. They entered the business world with copies of popular how-to books on being assertive tucked under their arms.

Now, these assertive women are being told to view themselves as victims. Gender feminism explains to these women that they cannot handle uncomfortable work situations without the protection of government. Like small children or the mentally disabled, they need a paternalistic state.

2. Women are losing their mentors. One of the main ways to advance in business or in academia is through the guidance of a mentor, who provides perspective and important contacts. A mentor naturally comes into close and friendly contact with the person being nurtured. As the charge of sexual harassment rears its litigious head, fewer and fewer men are willing to put their careers at risk by helping young women up the ladder.

At universities, many male professors are reluctant to advise female graduate students. Most of them are aware of colleagues who have defended themselves against charges of sexual misconduct. They realize that some of the evidence of sexual harassment—e.g., a late-night discussion over coffee—could have been used against them as well, even if their conduct was innocuous.

When these professors do accept female students, the women labor under disadvantages. For example, discussions may take place only during office hours with the door propped wide open, which allows for distractions. The women are often not invited to social events, which can be a vital part of networking. In order to protect themselves, male professors must approach female students with suspicion instead of goodwill.

3. *The emotional cost to men.* The most neglected cost of sexual harassment is the emotional duress it causes to men. This is neglected in two ways. First, men who are victims of sexual harassment are generally dismissed. Second, because they are seen to be in positions of power, men are assumed to be guilty until proven innocent. More and more, men report being paranoid about making innocent remarks and office relationships are becoming colder and less productive because of stilted communications. This is understandable. Men are now afraid to speak openly, make jokes, or compliment a woman on her dress. Every word and action might become evidence in a legal proceeding. To them, women's cry for decent treatment resembles nothing so much as a witch-hunt.

Sexual harassment is part of a war that gender feminists are waging against men. In her essay "Pluralist Myths and Powerless Men: The Ideology of Reasonableness in Sexual Harassment Law," Nancy S. Ehrenreich of the University of Denver explains how the rights of women are in direct conflict with those of men:

> It is logically incoherent to say that a group is free to pursue its own interest ... unless that conduct harms other groups.... *[A]ll* acts by any one group (or individual) are inevitably harmful to others. One side's freedom can always be seen as the other side's loss of security.[14]

Protecting women should not entail victimizing men.

Private Solutions to Sexual Harassment

Sexual harassment in the workplace is best resolved within the private sector, by the free market. Indeed, it has been argued that the problem is currently resolving itself through demographics. Gretchen Morgenson, a senior editor at *Forbes*, observed: "As women reach a critical mass in the work force, the problem of sexual harassment tends to go away. Freda

Klein says the problem practically vanishes once 30 percent of the workers in a department, an assembly line, or a company are women."[15]

Morgenson is optimistic about the future of working women—even the immediate future: "Reaching that critical mass won't take long. According to the Bureau of Labor Statistics, there will be 66 million women to 73 million men in the workplace by 2000."[16]

The first step toward solving sexual harassment is to view it in a realistic manner and to exclude behavior that is merely rude and offensive from its definition. Being offended is the price of living in society: it is part of the background noise everyone must tolerate as the price of freedom of speech.

True sexual harassment involves touching or behavior that makes it impossible to perform a job. Women can protect themselves from this behavior in several ways.

1. When the harassment is physical, women should be willing to press criminal charges, such as for assault or battery.

2. When the harassment is verbal, women must stop being victims and start standing up for themselves. On a face to face basis, they must confront verbal abuse and refuse to tolerate it.

3. Women should aggressively use the grievance procedures and remedies that almost every company of size has established. Most of the women who report harassment to researchers also admit that they never complained to their employers.

A key to resolving sexual harassment is to return it to the realm of tort law, which provides civil redress for private harms. The courts have a long history of viewing unwanted sexual contact as tortious—usually as a form of battery or assault. The law of torts, however, does not consider sexual comments and propositions to be actionable unless accompanied by a physical trespass against the victim's person.

Because the EEOC aims at preventing sexual discrimination in employment, it has tended to deemphasize the traditional role of tort law in providing relief from harm. Instead of pursuing remedies for individuals who have been actually injured, the EEOC seeks to regulate the workplace to prevent possible harm to an entire class of people.

Feminists also oppose the tort approach to sexual harassment. Catharine MacKinnon argues that torts miss the entire point of sexual harassment, which is not directed against an individual woman, but against women as a group. She explains that "the purpose of discrimination law is to change the society so that this kind of injury need not and does not recur. Tort law considers individual and compensable something which is fundamentally social."[17] Again, class rights are being used to deny rights to the individual.

Conclusion

The issue of sexual harassment has prompted a politically correct inquisition, with the goal of rooting out and punishing men who express attitudes deemed improper toward women. Its casualties are freedom of speech, the right to privacy, and the mechanism of the free market.

The fact that sexual harassment is ill-defined and poorly researched has not prevented it from impacting on society through the courts. This approach has disastrous costs, not the least of which is an escalation of the problem that causes harassment: the alienation of the sexes.

The law must not be used to enforce a feminist standard of virtue or to advance a political agenda that views men as the natural enemy of women.

Notes

1. *Liberty*, January 23, 1886.

2. *Time*, October 21, 1991.

3. *Sexual Harassment: A Report on the Sexual Harassment of Students* (Washington, D.C.: Report of the National Advisory Council of Women's Educational Programs, 1980), p. 7.

4. Nancy Tuana, "Sexual Harassment in Academe: Issues of Power and Coercion," in *Sexual Harassment: Confrontations and Decisions*, ed. Edmund Wall (Buffalo: Prometheus Books, 1992), p. 56.

5. Christina Hoff Sommers, *Who Stole Feminism?: How Women Have Betrayed Women* (New York: Simon & Schuster, 1994), pp. 114–115.

6. Kenneth C. Cooper, "The Six Levels of Sexual Harassment," *Contemporary Moral Controversies in Business*, ed. A. Pablo Iannone (New York: Oxford University Press, 1989), p. 190.

7. Ellen Frankel Paul, "Bared Buttocks and Federal Cases," *Society* 28, no. 4 (1991): 4–7.

8. Catharine MacKinnon, "Sexual Harassment as Sex Discrimination," in *Sexual Harassment: Confrontations and Decisions*, p. 145.

9. F. J. Tilly, *Sexual Harassment: A Report on the Sexual Harassment of Students* (Washington, D.C.: Report of the National Advisory Counsel of Women's Educational Programs, 1980), p. 7.

10. U.S. Merit Systems Protection Board, *Sexual Harassment in the Federal Workplace: Is It a Problem?* (Washington, D.C.: U.S. Government Printing Office, 1981). See also U.S. Merit Systems Protection Board, *Sexual Harassment in the Federal Government: An Update* (Washington, D.C.: U.S. Government Printing Office, 1988).

11. Sommers, *Who Stole Feminism?*, p. 183.

12. Gretchen Morgenson, "May I Have the Pleasure...," *National Review*, November 18, 1991, p. 37.

13. Hugh Davis Graham, *Civil Rights and the Presidency: Race and Gender in American Politics, 1960–1972* (New York: Oxford University Press, 1992), p. 223.

14. Nancy S. Ehrenreich, "Pluralistic Myths and Powerless Men," in *Sexual Harassment: Confrontations and Decisions*, p. 250.

15. Morgenson, "May I Have the Pleasure...," p. 41.

16. Ibid.

17. MacKinnon, "Sexual Harassment as Sex Discrimination," p. 144.

CHAPTER FIVE

Preferential Treatment of Women in Employment

One of the political issues the 1990s have inherited from the 1980s is that of preferential treatment of women in employment. Preference for women is considered necessary in order to afford us equal access to jobs and other opportunities from which we have been excluded for decades ... sometimes for centuries.

President Lyndon B. Johnson, architect of the Great Society, expressed this principle well in a statement that began with the words "Freedom is not enough." Johnson continued: "You do not take a person who for years has been hobbled by chains and liberate him, bring him up to the starting line of a race, and then say 'You're free to compete' and justly believe you have been completely fair."[1] Using "the gates of opportunity" as a metaphor, Johnson declared that it was not enough to open the gates. Every American citizen had to be able to walk through them.

Preferential policies address a wide spectrum of business situations, from job recruitment to pregnancy leave to adequate advancement for women. The literature surrounding such policies is immense. Conflicting statistics "prove" contradictory points of view. And the voices in the debate tend toward rhetoric rather than reason.

Perhaps the most fruitful approach to the preferential treatment of women is to return to the fundamental issues and principles underlying all policies of privilege based on gender. A good question to start with is: Where have these policies come from? What is the proximate cause of our current laws on the subject?

The Roots of Preference

During the social turbulence of the 1960s and '70s, reformers voiced a clear demand: discrimination must end! People must no longer be socially or economically slotted according to sex, race, or religion! The radical call for equality had the unmistakable ring of justice. The antidiscrimination cause gained popularity. After all, equal justice before the law and equal access to political power are well-entrenched American ideals.

But these were not the ideals being promoted. Traditionally, the concept of equal access to opportunity has been based on what is called a negative view of rights, which means that it is wrong to block anyone from exercising his or her right of self-ownership. This is embodied in the popular slogan from the American Revolution, "Don't Tread on Me" and in the famous French statement: "*Laissez faire. Laissez nous passez.*" (Let us be. Let us pass.) Negative rights are embodied in and expressed through laissez-faire capitalism.

The advocates of preference, however, are championing a comparatively new definition of equality into the American arena—that of social equality. They demand far more than the removal of legal barriers based on sex, and push for positive rights. This means that individuals and society have a duty to actively provide goods or services to others. The advocates of preference press for equal access to certain basic necessities, such as housing and education. Only by assuring basic needs to disadvantaged people, it was argued, could such people compete on an equal footing—in the case of women, with white males. In essence, the reformers proposed nothing less than a rough form of socioeconomic equality.

Where do women stand in this new social order? They are to be among the privileged because they—as a class—had suffered from discrimination. In his book, *New American Justice: Ending the White Male Monopolies*, Daniel C. Macguire declares: "This white male predominance has been institutionalized and legalized. Now, belatedly, it is being challenged. White males are responding with a vociferous reliance on 'meritocratic' ideals."[2]

White maleness has been institutionalized. Although virtually all legal barriers have been removed, it is claimed that the effects of the long-standing injustice are still evident. They still impact upon present generations of women. The lingering injustice is especially apparent in the marketplace, which continues to undervalue women's labor. The marketplace exploits the second-class status of women in society. Correcting this situation requires much more than the repeal of discriminatory laws; it requires the institution of laws and policies that actively prefer women. Only by being preferred can women be equal.

Myra K. Wolfgang, speaking as a member of the Michigan Women's Commission, expressed this well: "We, who want equal opportunities, equal pay for equal work and equal status for women, know that frequently we obtain real equality through a difference in treatment, rather than identity in treatment."[3]

Institutional Analysis

During the 1960s and '70s, a political phrase became popular, "institutional discrimination." This phrase referred to institutional arrangements that excluded or hindered certain classes of people from participating in the distribution of power. The phrase reflected the general drift away from the traditionally American emphasis on individual responsibility and toward a left-wing condemnation of the free-market system.

Feminists used the idea of institutional discrimination to explain why women seemed to be excluded from various occupations and why they were paid less. Institutional discrimination was distinguished from personal prejudice. Even a company with no bias against women would discriminate against them simply because it operated in the context of patriarchy.

For example, a company with community spirit may confine its hiring to its local area, in which there may be no qualified women. This effectively prevents a woman from competing for positions in this company. Thus, from such a laudable motive as civic pride, the company is guilty of institutional discrimination. The key to determine whether or not discrimination has occurred is not the intention of the company but how it apportioned its power and opportunities. Only one method of apportionment and one result—that of social equality—is considered justified.

What Is Justice? Paternalism versus Freedom

At the heart of this issue is the question of how power—economic, social, or political—should be distributed. What constitutes justice? How is it achieved? Here the gender feminist concept of justice is in direct conflict with the individualist feminist one.

To individualists, the freely chosen actions of every person must be respected. Thus, their view of justice is "means-oriented." That is, individualist feminists claim that as long as a social situation is nonviolent and voluntary, it is just. Justice is not a matter of achieving a particular end-state, such as equality or nondiscrimination. Justice refers to a *process* that respects the self-ownership of every person in society. If no rights are violated, justice has been achieved.

This is not to say that a perfect society would result. Nor does it deny the importance of other social virtues such as charity or compassion. It *is* to say that the best we can do is to respect other people's choices and demand that same respect in return.

In contrast, the gender feminists' concept of justice is "ends-oriented." The end is social, economic, and political equality for women. And virtually any means—including the use of law and force to regulate attitudes and peaceful behavior—is justified as long as it results in their version of justice. Gender feminists may cry out against discrimination, but they are not above using it for their own purposes.

As gender feminist Catharine MacKinnon explains in *Feminism Unmodified*: "In this analysis, both Marxism and feminism are theories of power, of its unequal distribution. They each provide an account of how a systematically unequal social arrangement is internally coherent and internally rational and pervasive, yet unjust."[4]

The noble cause to which discrimination is put is "the protection of women." Gender feminists call upon the state to abrogate freedom of speech and most economic freedoms in order to protect women, who are seen as weak and oppressed. There is a word that describes the state's interference in society in order to benefit or protect a weak group from exploitation: paternalism. This term is most often associated with children and the mentally incompetent. Now gender feminists want to throw paternalism over women like a blanket—or a straitjacket.

Paternalism often expresses itself in a form of puritanism. This is a logical development. In order to protect the interests of a particular group, the government must assess what is "good" and what is "bad" for that group. The state version of "good" becomes institutionalized; its version of "bad" is prohibited. "Goods," such as equal access to the wealth of others (e.g., in the form of equal employment laws) become mandatory. "Bads," such as discrimination, become punishable offenses.

The Free Market versus State Action

Anyone who thinks the free market should be regulated by government should answer the following fundamental question: do you see any real difference between someone who offers you money for something you own (such as your labor) and someone who puts a gun to your head to demand the same thing? Do you see a fundamental difference between a voluntary exchange and a coerced one? And if you do, which seems preferable?

To translate this question into more relevant terms: given that an employer owns the resources he or she is allocating and that you own your labor, do you believe that the two of you should be allowed to negotiate freely? Or should a third party with no ownership stake—such as the government—be able to dictate the terms of the contract? Most people would favor economic freedom and respect for private property. Most people believe that you have the right to sell what you own (including your labor) at whatever price you are willing to accept.

Now change the scenario slightly. Imagine the employer is offering you a "bad" deal, which you accept only because you are in financial need. Also imagine that the third party intends to intervene on your behalf to assure what it considers to be "good" for you, such as the minimum wage. Would you still advocate economic freedom? Or would you consider the intervention to be justified? In other words, do you believe that you should be economically free only to make good decisions and not bad ones?

Individualist feminists maintain that any exchange that occurs voluntarily is more fair than one that is coerced. Gender feminists turn to government to guarantee their version of fairness through force of law.

Statistical Analysis

Before dealing directly with the arguments, however, it is necessary to address the related issue of statistical analysis. Social planning has been called the stepchild of statistical analysis. The "technology of social measurement" has been, perhaps, the most powerful weapon used by advocates of preference. Indeed, social indicators have been used as the standard to identify whether or not institutional discrimination exists in any particular situation. Yet, many critics believe it is impossible to measure qualitative as opposed to quantitative differences. Such skepticism is embodied in the old common saying, "You can't compare apples with oranges."

A quantitative difference is embodied in the price of apples and oranges. If on a given day you are willing to pay $1 for an apple and only 50 cents for an orange, you might be said to like apples (at that moment) twice as much as you like oranges. But a qualitative difference—even in a simple comparison between two fruits—is far more difficult to assess, let alone predict. If apples become more expensive, do you then prefer oranges? What if you have eaten an apple every day for two weeks in a row? What if the purpose of your purchase is to make juice for breakfast?

Moving on to qualitative comparisons—such as marriage versus bachelorhood, compassion versus justice—dramatizes how impossible real measurement may be, especially since *all* social scientists have biases or agendas that influence the objectivity of their statistics. Howard Sherman, in his book *Radical Political Economy*, explains, "No social scientist is unbiased; all come from a particular social environment, and all have tentative conclusions (conscious or unconscious) on any issue they are investigating."[5]

Sherman does not consider such bias, if honestly reported, to be a negative factor. "A social science that presented no conclusions would be useless. Imagine an engineer who tells us there are ten different ways to build the bridge we are considering, but refuses to tell us which he believes best under the circumstances."[6] A problem arises, however, when studies are presented as objective and factual, without acknowledgment of their biases.

The problems of statistical analysis are well documented. Statistics attempt to measure elusive and vague factors, such as opportunity; they generalize from particulars and they contain the assumptions of the analysts. Moreover, statistics do not bring a context or a perspective to the raw data. For example, statistics revealing that women's wages rose after a piece of legislation was passed do not indicate if the wages were rising before the legislation; perhaps the rate of increase actually slowed. Nor do statistics offer any sense of cause and effect. By the time statistics are accumulated, processed, and converted into policy they may well be out-of-date.

Nevertheless, social planners use statistical analysis as though it provided unimpeachable knowledge and as though it were value-free. Backed by truckloads of statistics, they propose to regulate the attitudes and behavior of society—especially of the business community. Their goal: equality. Equal opportunity for the disadvantaged is to be mandated—if not by law, then by the threat of court action.

The General Arguments for Equality

In general, three arguments are used to justify the preferential treatment of women in employment. They are: (1) utilitarian or arguments for the social good; (2) arguments for compensatory justice, usually based on historical injustice; and (3) arguments for the ideal of equality.

First, the utilitarian argument. According to this line of reasoning, society will be enriched by preferring women and allowing them to achieve equality. There are several ways to critique this argument. You could point out that utilitarian or pragmatic considerations tend to blow in the wind of circumstance; they change with each freshly elected administration, with every economic shift, and with many world events, such as declaration of war. To base the ideal of equality on the argument for utility is to lay a foundation of sand.

As well, you could speculate on the long-term consequences to society of using a quota system rather than individual merit as the standard by which to allocate jobs and wealth. Preferential policies inevitably drive a wedge between individual worth and economic success. It is difficult to understand how this wedge enriches society.

But another critique of the utilitarian argument strikes more at the heart of preferential policies. It examines, in human terms, the costs and risks of forcing employers to prefer women simply because they are women. One cost is that those groups who are being discriminated against—in this case men—will be understandably resentful, and they will translate their resentment into a heightened sexism. Instead of being overt, the new sexism will be subtle and covert. It will be less open to remedy through education and persuasion.

In his essay "Race Unconsciousness and the White Male," Frederick R. Lynch quotes some census data:

> From 1976 to 1984 the median white male's inflation-adjusted income (in 1984 dollars) declined 22 percent to $16,467 from $21,175. This decline cannot be traced to inflation or a falling gross national product, since over the same period of time the real GNP has risen 26 percent.[7]

The effect of preferential policies for women could be equally devastating. In rushing to appear unbiased, employers will tend to promote women prematurely into jobs they are not prepared to handle. Or they will promote women into whatever vacancies occur within the company, whether or not the women have the necessary background. When these women fail or perform in a mediocre manner, men will see this as confirmation that women cannot handle high-level positions.

What will be the effect on women who advance through merit and hard work? A de facto quota system preferring women will stigmatize every woman in the work force as inferior. In years past, it was assumed

that women succeeded in business by sleeping with the boss; now it will
be assumed that they succeed by virtue of political privilege. The woman
who achieves excellence on her own will never receive the recognition
she deserves.

In essence, preferential policies will increase the very prejudice (sexism) they seek to eliminate at the expense of the very group (women)
they seek to benefit. This is the cost. And it contradicts a major assumption underlying the utilitarian approach, namely, that wealth and power
can simply be transferred from one group to another. Advocates of preference assume that the transfer of wealth and power is a zero-sum game.
The contrary is true. It is quite possible and, indeed, probable that everyone will lose. This is the risk.

But even disregarding the above objections, it is difficult to imagine
how the utilitarian argument for preference lives up to its own standards. For example, can it be implemented? The question becomes: Is it
possible to control a massively complex and ever shifting set of social
interactions? After all, people and society respond in unpredictable ways.
In his book *Preferential Policies*, the black economist Thomas Sowell has
observed: "Those who initiate preferential policies cannot sufficiently control the reactions of either preferred or non-preferred groups to ensure
that such policies will have the desired effect ... in the desired direction."[8]

Consider just one aspect of what would be required to regulate the
fairness of employment: it would require a vast and constant flow of knowledge. It would require constant input to reflect moment by moment
changes in the economic situation. It would also assume a context for
this knowledge, part of which would be a good picture of what nondiscrimination looks like. Only by referring to this picture could you tell
when a situation was deviating from it that is, whether or not it was discriminatory. Advocates of preference tend to assume that nondiscrimination would naturally result if prejudice were swept away. Employment
would accurately reflect the overall ratio of men to women, whites to
blacks, etc. To find discrimination, they look for deviations from this ideal
pattern.

But does such a deviation constitute discrimination? It might result
from such unrelated factors as the age spread of a given community or
its geography. Any particular disparity may well be accidental or be caused
by something unrelated to discrimination.

Of course, each disparity from the pattern could be judged on case
by case, but this would involve such a bureaucratic nightmare that no
one suggests this alternative. The attitude seems to be that it is better

for the innocent to suffer than the guilty to go free. This attitude is embodied in the fact that companies who are sued must prove that no discrimination occurred. They are no longer innocent until proven guilty.

Second, the argument for compensatory justice. In law, this principle requires anyone causing an injury to another person must rectify the damage. The innocent party must receive compensation. Advocates of preference go one step further, claiming that the descendants of those injured must receive compensation as well. After all, it is argued, the descendants are still living with the consequences of centuries of discrimination. For example, the low socioeconomic status forced upon a woman's mother may have deprived the daughter of a university education. This argument boils down to a call for righting historical wrongs.

Objections to the argument for the state as remedial historian are myriad. One of the more basic ones is that it is not possible to rectify past injustices when the injured parties are dead.

My objections to the use of preferential policies to correct historical wrongs fall into two categories: (1) the people receiving the benefits are not victims, and (2) the people forced to provide the compensation have done no wrong.

1. The women who receive the benefits of preferential policies are not the same women who suffered the centuries of injustice. The simple fact of human mortality assures this point. In essence, it is impossible to rewrite human history.

Advocates of preference argue, however, that the present generation of women still suffers from the shadow of history. For example, it is claimed that the alleged underrepresentation of women in the medical profession bears a direct relationship to the original injustice of barring them from this field. Thus, the heirs (at least, the female heirs) of victimized women have a valid claim to compensation.

This carries the theory of compensatory justice far beyond conventional legal practice. Even the groundbreaking compensation granted to victims of so great a tragedy as the Holocaust did not encompass payments to future generations. The compensation embodied in preferential policies is open-ended with no possible limit to the amount owed by the guilty party.

To demand compensation for the grandchildren of victims is to confuse a justifiable sense of compassion with a legal claim. Present generations are undoubtedly influenced by many things that happened to their ancestors. But this is a matter of causality, not of morality. The class into which you are born—whether defined by sex, race, or social status—is an accident of nature. Even John Rawls, an advocate of distributive justice, concedes: "The natural distribution is neither just nor unjust; nor is it unjust that persons are born into society at some particular position. These are simply natural facts."[9] However, as Rawls continues, "What is just and unjust is the way that institutions deal with these facts."[10]

The question remains: If there is no injustice, how can there be a legal claim for compensation? If the natural distribution of wealth and opportunity is neither just nor unjust, then what happens to the moral underpinning of the crusade for socioeconomic equality?

There is an interesting question that bears on this moral underpinning. Indeed, it can be used as a litmus test of whether or not advocates of preference are sincere about righting past history. The question is: What of the women of privilege? Are women from the Rockefeller family, for instance, to be given preferential treatment along with the descendants of blue-collar, working-class women? If compensation is the goal, then the women who have been victimized should be preferred, not those women who benefited from the oppression.

A policy of preferring only disadvantaged and not wealthy ones has never been seriously proposed. This fact alone sheds doubt on the much trumpeted goal of fighting for the underdog. At this point, the advocate of preference begins to look like just another advocate of government control. Gender equality begins to look like just another political grab at the wealth of society.

2. The people forced to pay the compensation have done no wrong.[11] Guilt cannot be inherited. H. A. Deane in *Justice: Compensatory and Distributive*, observes:

> Present members of the society are being asked to assume the responsibility not only for unjust acts in the present or the recent past in which they may have had no share, but also for acts of discrimination which were performed long before they were born.[12]

Deane points to a final irony confronting white males who are made to suffer for the wrongs of American history: "Indeed, their fathers and grandfathers may not have been Americans at all but may have been suffering persecution and discrimination, for example, in Eastern Europe."[13] Further, it is unjust to hold every member in a class of people—such as men—responsible for actions in which they had no part as individuals.

Perhaps the best overall critique of the argument for compensatory justice has been presented by Thomas Sowell in his book *Preferential Policies*:

> Given the mortality of human beings, often the only compensation for historic wrongs that is within the scope of our knowledge and control is

purely symbolic compensation—taking from individuals who inflicted no harm and giving to individuals who suffered none.[14]

Third: the argument for the ideal of equality. Equality is an ambiguous word. People who use the word frequently mean different and contrary things by it. To some, any difference at all between human beings—social, physical, economic, etc.—constitutes an inequality. Others contend that such differences are natural or even healthy. This attitude is embodied in the phrases "different but equal" or "separate but equal."

Two examples of humans being different but equal are the differences between those with brown and those with blue eyes. A difference becomes an inequality only when a normative judgment is attached. Thus, if I say, "people with blue eyes are superior," then having brown eyes ceases to be a difference and becomes an inequality. Discrimination and inequality exist only in the context of comparing one class with another. The salient question for any definition of equality thus is: When does a difference become an inequality?

Traditionally, American society has considered differences *before the law* or *in access to political power* to be inequalities. This definition focuses on the individual in relationship to the state and grants that: every individual should be free to pursue happiness, wealth, and well-being to the extent of his or her abilities to do so.

Advocates of preference have a different definition of equality. Even in the absence of legal or political barriers, they consider any difference in the access of groups or classes to private wealth and private power to constitute an inequality. This definition focuses on the rights of certain classes (women or employees) as they relate to other classes (men or employers). This concept of equality is based on socioeconomics and class theory; it seeks to redistribute the wealth and power of society, usually through imposing state control on erring individuals. Thus, the definition of equality used by advocates of preference bears no resemblance to that used by advocates of individual rights. Indeed, they are incompatible on several points.

First, advocates of preference divide society into classes rather than viewing it as a collection of individuals. No distinction is made between innocent or guilty individuals—privileged or victimized women because people are innocent or guilty by virtue of the class to which they belong. This is profoundly unindividualistic and antagonistic to individual rights.

Second, preferential policies reverse the traditional American safeguard of liberty—the protection of the rights of the individual against intrusion by the state. Instead, the state becomes the arbiter of justice in the conflicts between two classes of society. Perhaps this is a consequence of the belief that the law should function as a remedial historian and as a social analyst.

This is in stark contrast to the established view of laws as existing to protect individuals and their property from violence. Now the purview of the law has been expanded to include, for example, the refusal to hire someone. In essence, the law is used to impose morality rather than merely to enforce the peace.

Third, policies of preference in employment constitute an attempt to destroy the traditional free-market system. Through preferential policies government becomes involved, to an unprecedented degree, in business decisions. This involvement constitutes control, and thus, it is a major step toward state-control of privately owned business—the designation for such a political system is fascism.

The Free Market as an Arena of Equality

The final irony is that the surest safeguard against discrimination is the very mechanism that is being destroyed—the free market. Historically, the free market has tended to eliminate discrimination simply because this practice costs companies money. Discrimination reduces the pool of talent from which employees can be drawn, it alienates customers, on whose patronage companies depend, and it lowers the efficiency of production since trained employees will not put up with discrimination, but will seek advancement elsewhere. Thus, the free market—in pursuit of profit—has tended to advance individual talent, regardless of the person's sex or race.

What is the record of the state on discrimination? Consider the case of racial discrimination in the American South. The civil-rights movement arose in protest to an elderly black woman's arrest for sitting in the front of a bus in Montgomery, Alabama. What role did the bus company play in this drama? Jim Crow laws—laws discriminating against blacks—had been part of Southern history for decades. Many bus companies refused to enforce them. For some companies, this may have been a moral stand; more likely, the bus companies simply did not wish to alienate black customers by forcing them to sit in the back. The streetcar company in Montgomery was among those who refused to discriminate. It reasoned that a customer is a customer. Only when streetcar conductors were arrested for nondiscrimination did the bus companies comply with the law.

A similar and more general observation may be made of Jim Crow laws in the South. The state, and not the free market, was responsible for institutionalized injustice. In his book *Forbidden Ground: The Case Against Employment Discrimination Laws*, Richard Epstein describes the true lesson of segregation:

> The dominant evil in the pre-1964 period was not self-interest or markets, inflexible human nature, or even bigotry. It was excessive state power and the pattern of private violence, intimidation, and lynching, of which there is painful record but against which there was no effective federal remedy.[15]

In short, racism in the South was bolstered by state laws rather than by the recognition of individual rights: "The explicit discrimination in the South and elsewhere was preserved by the use of coercion, both by state law and by private individuals (such as the Ku Klux Klan) whose activities were left unchecked by state agents."[16] State laws prevented sympathetic whites from employing or otherwise associating with blacks, just as laws against emancipation a century before had prevented many whites from freeing their slaves.

Although prejudiced individuals could have shut blacks or women out of the marketplace in certain areas, other opportunities would have always opened up for them. This is because those who refuse to do business because of other people's race or sex pay a high price in terms of profits and lost opportunities. For example, imagine an American businessman who refuses to deal with the Japanese because he "remembers" Pearl Harbor. He would place himself at a competitive disadvantage. It is only through the state that discrimination can be institutionalized and maintained by force.

This is not to say that the marketplace is less prejudiced than the community in which it operates. But it does function on the basis of different principles; it exists to make a profit. Thus, the free market—which is color- and sex-blind to the source of its income—is a great leveler of inequality.

Conclusion

The preferential treatment of women in employment is nothing less than an attack on the rights of the individual and the free market. The demand for socioeconomic equality runs against an ingrained sense of fairness; it runs against the sense that every individual has the right to the fruits of whatever talent or resource he or she possesses.

Preferential policies can be likened to the shackling of the best runners at the beginning of a race so that no one can excel. It is not clear how such a policy can advance the well-being of society.

Notes

1. Address to graduating class, Howard University, June 4, 1965, as cited in Thomas Dye, *Understanding Public Policy*, 2d ed. (Englewood Cliffs, N.J.: Prentice-Hall, 1975), p. 62.

2. Daniel C. Macguire, *New American Justice: Ending the White Male Monopolies* (Garden City, N.Y.: Doubleday, 1980), p. 3.

3. As quoted in *America's Working Women: A Documentary History, 1600 to the Present* (New York: Vintage Books, 1976), p. 378.

4. MacKinnon, *Feminism Unmodified*, p. 49.

5. Howard Sherman, *Radical Political Economy: Capitalism and Socialism from a Marxist-Humanist Perspective* (New York: Basic Books, 1972), p. 6.

6. Ibid.

7. Frederick R. Lynch, "Race Unconsciousness and the White Male," *Society* (Jan/Feb 1992), p. 31.

8. Thomas Sowell, *Preferential Policies: An International Perspective* (New York: Morrow, 1990), p. 124.

9. John Rawls, *A Theory of Justice* (Cambridge: Harvard University Press, 1971), p. 102.

10. Ibid.

11. By the word "pay," I refer not only to taxpayers, but to those men who are discriminated against and those business people who must submit to government regulation.

12. H. A. Deane, *Justice: Compensatory and Distributive* (New York: Columbia University, 1974), pp. 13–14.

13. Ibid.

14. Sowell, *Preferential Policies*, p. 160.

15. Richard Epstein, *Forbidden Ground: The Case Against Employment Discrimination Laws* (Cambridge, Mass.: Harvard University Press, 1992), p. 93.

16. Ibid.

CHAPTER SIX

What Does Affirmative Action Affirm?

Affirmative action has been a debacle. It has not cured sex segregation in the workplace or closed the wage gap between men and women. More importantly, by taking choice from individuals and entrusting it to social planners, it has hindered the institution that has done the most to benefit women economically: the free market.

Real Life

A friend of mine was recently passed over for tenure at an Ivy League school. This was surprising to me; he had been teaching at the university for several years and was immensely popular, not only with the students but also within the department. With a book and several journal articles to his credit, his qualifications were in good order. So what was the problem?

He explained it to me: he was a white male in a department that needed more visible women and minorities. Never mind that the woman hired had less experience and fewer credentials. Never mind that the university had been grooming him for the position—indeed, the department head could not even look him in the eyes when breaking the news. Never mind that my friend is now so embittered that he tells his male students to forget pursuing a degree in the humanities, because credentials and quality do not matter anymore. If they are white and male, he insists, there will be no place for them in academia.

I hope he is overstating the case, but he is understandably bitter; it is difficult not to rail against unfairness when there is next to no recourse against it.

If my friend were a woman, he could sue the university for unfair employment practices under Title VII of the Civil Rights Act of 1964. This section of the act states that it is unlawful for any employer: "(1) to fail or refuse to hire or discharge any individual, or otherwise to discriminate against any individual with respect to his compensation, terms, or privileges of employment because of such individual's race, color, religion, sex or national origin."

But to bring such a suit he would have to belong to a class protected by Title VII, that is, he would have to be a woman or a minority. As a male of German-Irish ancestry, he is not simply excluded from protection; he is, in fact, the person against whom protection is being offered. Why is this protection necessary? My friend has always been sex-blind when it comes to his students and colleagues. Why, then, do women have to be shielded from him?

Because, it is argued, women have historically been discriminated against in employment. Since white males (as a class) have benefited from this injustice, they must now (as a class) bear the brunt of adjusting the balance. This includes him. In her book *Feminism Unmodified*, Catharine MacKinnon explains why my friend is inescapably my oppressor: "The social relation between the sexes is organized so that men may dominate and women must submit and this relation is sexual."[1]

What Is Affirmative Action?

The contradictory notion of discriminating in order to obtain equal treatment seems to violate common sense. This contradiction leads wayward feminists, like me, to ask: What exactly is affirmative action? And what is being affirmed?

Affirmative action, as a policy, is usually said to be in effect when a company or an institution takes reasonable action to remedy any discriminatory behavior that has occurred in the past. On ethical grounds, most people would agree with such a policy although many would question the wisdom of enforcing the policy by law.

The spirit of affirmative action seems different from a literal interpretation of the policy's words, however. To understand this spirit it is necessary to examine the roots of the issue in the context of the feminist movement from which affirmative action sprang.

First, it is necessary to acknowledge the truth of affirmative action's main claim: historically, women have been the victims of discrimination. Until early in the twentieth century women were excluded from universities and unions, barred from professions such as medicine, and—upon marriage—they often lost all title to whatever pittance they were allowed to earn. During the twentieth century, the legal barriers confronting women began, one by one, to fall. Vestiges of legal inequality still exist, but the instances are few—e.g., women and men often receive different sentences for the same crime. And in many cases these differences are beginning to favor women at the expense of men.

The cry for affirmative action makes no sense if the goal is simply equal treatment before the law. Affirmative action, however, is based on the concept of socioeconomic equality, which became popular during the 1960s. Access to the basic necessities was presented as the right of every American. The fact that the law was to allocate these goods on a favored basis to certain classes of Americans, such as blacks and women, was justified on two grounds. First, they were the victims of another class of Americans: white males. Second, only by assuring equal access to such goods as education could the disadvantaged compete fairly.

What of women in this new world? Although legal barriers to women had largely fallen, it was argued that the ill effects of history still affected modern women. The lingering injustice was especially blatant in the marketplace, which continued to undervalue women's work. The removal of legal barriers had not cured this exploitation; the institution of legal protection was required. It was necessary for the law to prefer women in order for the marketplace to treat them fairly.

Affirmative action policies prefer women through a wide range of measures, including remedial training, lower required scores on tests for jobs or university admission, recruitment procedures aimed at women, and child care facilities.

Why should an employer accept these measures? Basically, there are two reasons. First, although affirmative action has seldom been mandated by law, administrative regulations and judicial rulings have often lent this policy the force of law. In 1965 President Lyndon B. Johnson established the Office of Federal Contract Compliance, which ensured that private businesses who did work for the federal government followed nondiscrimination requirements. As a result, a large block of the American economy adopted affirmative action. Under the federal guidelines of 1971 statistical representation became the litmus test of discrimination.

On a more local level, most states have Fair Employment Practice Laws and civil rights agencies that enforce them. Among the damages that can be awarded are hiring or reinstatement, promotion, training, seniority, a pay increase, back pay, which is broadly defined to include pension and educational benefits, and legal fees.

The second reason why an employer would accept these requirements is that the cost of swimming against affirmative action can be very high. In 1980, for example, a court ordered the Ford Motor Company to give $13 million in back pay to women and minorities. Attorney fees alone can bankrupt a company. In a sex discrimination case against the University of Minnesota, the attorney fees came to $1,475,000. The successful plaintiff later abandoned academia to become a lawyer.

Even companies rigidly implementing affirmative action policies are not safe from the litigation surrounding this issue. For example, Sears and Roebuck was one of the first large companies to voluntarily develop an affirmative action plan. The company was also among the first to be sued by the government, who used Sears' own statistics to show that women were underrepresented as salespersons of such commodities as automobile tires. Sears was eventually exonerated. Ironically, it became a target largely because its records on affirmative action were meticulously kept and available for inspection. Its attempt to comply backfired badly.

Thus, the marketplace—in self-defense—has adopted a de facto quota system to protect itself against charges of discrimination. How, in the name of fairness, have we arrived at a system that openly discriminates on the basis of sex?

Arguments for Affirmative Action

To recap from the previous chapter: three arguments have been offered (1) social good; (2) compensatory justice; and (3) equality.

The social good, or utilitarian, argument states that society will be enriched by advancing women. This is a relatively lightweight justification, since advocates of affirmative action themselves generally concede that they would push equality even if it were to the detriment of society. Moreover, it is easy to point out the disastrous long-term consequences to society of using a quota system rather than merit to allocate jobs. Affirmative action drives a wedge between individual worth and economic success: how does this benefit society?

Indeed, affirmative action might well increase the very evil it seeks to cure, prejudice. In his book *Illiberal Education*, D'Souza remarks on a strange phenomenon occurring on campuses across America. Although student attitudes on race have grown more informed, incidents of racial hostility on campuses seem to be increasing. D'Souza concludes that a new kind of racism is appearing, one that has been created by affirmative action—that is, by the legal preference given to blacks. This racism stems from the understandable resentment felt by white or Oriental students. It is a prejudice that springs, not from ignorance, but from experience.

Women in the workplace face a similar dilemma. In order to fill their quotas, employers may promote women too quickly or into inappropriate departments. When these women fail, that failure will be seen as confirmation of the inadequacy of their sex. When women succeed on their own merit, many people assume their success was due to preferential policies and was undeserved. And what of the men who are discriminated against? Their understandable resentment might well be translated into a heightened sexism—just as my friend's rejection has embittered him toward all of academia.

The black free-market economist Thomas Sowell has commented on the bitter irony of blacks who had succeeded on their own merit being victimized by preferential policies because they are not given due credit for their accomplishments. The same is true of women in the marketplace. In short, affirmative action is not what economists call a zero-sum game, by which wealth and power are simply transferred from one group to another. It is possible for everyone to be a loser in the exchange.

The argument from compensatory justice claims that anyone who causes injury to an innocent person should remedy the damage. Affirmative action goes one step farther, however, and claims that descendants of the injured parties deserve compensation as well. There are two basic objections to this argument: the people receiving compensation are not the victims; and, the people being forced to pay the compensation have done nothing wrong.[2]

Indeed, many of those forced to pay are also victims of historical prejudice. Sowell comments on this further irony:

> The fact that some groups are poor because of historical injustices done to them has been taken by many as a blank check to consider all lower income groups victims of injustice. In many parts of the world, however, those initially in dire poverty have, over the generations, raised themselves to an above-average level of prosperity, by great effort and painful sacrifice. Now the deep thinkers come along and want to redistribute what they earn to others who were initially more fortunate but less hard working.[3]

The third most common argument for preferential treatment is a moral one, based on the ideal of equality.[4] Yet government, in all its forms and on an international basis, has an abysmal record where equality is concerned. It was not Henry Ford who inscribed the institution of slavery into the Constitution; it was politicians. Gary S. Becker, in his book *The Economics of Discrimination*, emphasizes the role of the government and of those who would use government in oppressing minorities. He uses what is, perhaps, the most notorious case of discrimination to illustrate his point, namely, South Africa: "Early in the twentieth century the government of South Africa already restricted the employment of blacks in mines—largely, it should be added, at the urging of the union of white miners."[5]

Becker continues with an impressive list of government-induced racism, including

> the confiscation of some property of Japanese Americans in the United States during World War II, the restrictions legislated against Negroes in various Southern states, the limited amount of public education available to Jews in eastern Europe for several centuries, or the government-imposed apartheid in South Africa.[6]

A Good Word for Discrimination

Self-ownership—a woman's body, a woman's right—requires the right to discrimination. To own something means to control its use, including the right of "freedom of association," the right to freely choose your friends and your employees on the basis of your own standards and judgment.

But freedom has risks. One of them is that people may choose to deal with women in a biased and offensive manner. As long as this discrimination is peaceful—that is, it involves no physical injury or threat of harm—it is not a violation of rights. Such discrimination is simply ignorant behavior, which shows incredibly poor taste. But both freedom of speech and freedom of association guarantee that people have the right to be wrong, to be offensive, to be prejudiced. Freedom of association requires the right to say no and to refuse to associate.

Indeed, discrimination, on some level, occurs in everyone's life. It is an inescapable part of forming preferences and tastes. As Gary Becker observes:

> Discrimination and prejudice are not usually said to occur when someone prefers looking at a glamorous Hollywood actress rather than at some other woman; yet they are said to occur when he prefers living next to whites rather than next to Negroes.[7]

Everyone reaches his or her own conclusions about other people. And, in general, people associate with those they favor and avoid those they consider objectionable—for whatever reason. We invite friends into our homes and bar those who seem unpleasant to us. In the same manner, people have the right to hire whomever they consider appropriate. The decision may be biased; it may be "wrong," by society's standards, but a free society allows individuals to make their own judgments and allocate their own resources.

Discriminating on the basis of gender may well be unjust. But even in this case, women will benefit more from a free-market system than from government regulation. Even if a hefty percentage of society is misogynist, there will always be many others who want to profit by doing business with women. Any discrimination that is suffered will be random and escapable.

In his book, *Forbidden Ground: The Case Against Employment Discrimination Laws*, Richard Epstein observes that "In a world in which 90% of the people are opposed to doing business with me, I shall concentrate my attention on doing business with the other 10%."[8]

He explains that as long as individual rights are respected, racism or sexism will have only a limited impact: "as long as the tort law is in place, my enemies are powerless to block out mutually beneficial transaction by their use of force.... The critical question for my welfare is not which opportunities are lost but which are retained."[9]

Conclusion

The government's attempt to regulate the peaceful behavior and attitudes of society is doomed. It is ridiculous to suppose that the complex, ever-shifting interactions of society can be controlled. Even one of the most totalitarian governments, that of the Soviet Union, was unable to prevent market forces and personal preferences from erupting in the form of the black market.

The consequences of affirmative action cannot be controlled or even predicted. This is because the individuals involved—both the perceived beneficiaries and losers—are not automatons. They are not, in Thomas Sowell's words, "blocks of wood passively placed where the policy dictates."

Unfortunately, theorizing can bring little solace to my friend, who is debating whether or not to abandon the one career that has ever meant anything to him. There is no encouragement I can give him. What he says is true: no matter how good he is or how much he cares, doors are slammed in his face because he is a white male.

Equality means equal treatment, not privilege. Caring for those who suffer means caring for men as well as women. Justice requires that all human beings receive what they individually deserve. So far, all I have seen of affirmative action is institutionalized discrimination and sloppy thinking.

Notes

1. MacKinnon, *Feminism Unmodified*, p. 16.
2. For an in-depth discussion of these objections, please see chapter 5, "Preferential Treatment of Women in Employment."
3. Thomas Sowell, *Compassion versus Justice*, p. 30.
4. See chapter 5 for in-depth treatment.
5. Gary S. Becker, *The Economics of Discrimination* (Chicago: University of Chicago Press, 1971), p. 7.
6. Ibid.
7. Ibid., p. 13.
8. Epstein, *Forbidden Ground*, p. 30.
9. Ibid.

CHAPTER SEVEN

Comparable Worth

Comparable worth, sometimes called pay equity, is the policy that declares women should be paid the same amount as men for performing jobs of comparable value. This is different from maintaining that men and women doing the *same* job should receive equal pay. Comparable worth involves ranking a wide range of jobs and deciding which ones have the same value. According to the law in Washington State, comparable worth entails providing women with "similar salaries for positions that require or impose similar responsibilities, judgments, knowledge, skills and working conditions [as men]."[1] The two questions that set the intellectual foundation of this issue are: Why are women paid less than men? and What—if anything—should be done about the disparity?

Background

The drive for comparable worth has been fueled by the failure of '60s feminism to better the overall economic status of women. During the '60s, feminists aimed at eliminating two economic evils, the wage gap— the difference between what women and men earned—and sex segregation in the workplace. The goals of these feminists were simple, they wanted women to earn as much as men, and they wanted equal access to jobs of all descriptions. In 1963 the Equal Pay Act ordered employers to pay women the same as they paid men when both were performing equal work. In theory, the wage gap should have disappeared; in reality, it remained virtually unchanged.

Feminists then pointed to sex segregation as the problem. The Civil Rights Act of 1964 was interpreted to prohibit discriminatory employment practices, including the refusal to promote or hire women for high-paying jobs. The result was affirmative action, and it was meant to eliminate sex segregation, by which women were channeled into low-level jobs, called pink-collar ghettos. After two decades of this social policy, the wage gap should have disappeared, but it has remained virtually unchanged.

Why? In the introduction to the book *Wage Justice*, Catherine R. Stimpson explains that "Despite new laws that embodied this belief, women's wages kept on being significantly less than those of men. One reason for the doggedness of the gap is the fact that many men and women still do not do the same sort of work."[2]

In other words, affirmative action had failed. The wage gap remained because women still tended to hold lower-level jobs that paid less. They became secretaries instead of engineers, nurses instead of doctors. Women were trapped in the cycle of being paid less because they performed women's jobs, which, in turn, paid less because they were done by women. Bridging the wage gap required far more than affirmative action or "equal pay for equal work" legislation. It required that feminists accomplish one of two goals: either eliminate sex segregation by some means, such as a new form of affirmative action or make "women's work" somehow pay as well as men's work. That "somehow" became the policy of comparable worth.

In essence, gender feminists gave up on eliminating sex segregation and focused instead on making women's work more remunerative. In her book, *Doing Comparable Worth: Gender, Class, and Pay Equity*, gender feminist Joan Acker explains why sex segregation seemed inevitable: "A central theme of this book is that gender inequalities seem to be so deeply embedded in social structures and processes that they are recreated even as we try to eliminate them. Differences between the sexes are reconstituted in new guises."[3]

Instead of demanding equal pay for equal work, feminists now demanded "equal pay for comparable work." This meant that seemingly unrelated jobs had to be evaluated according to various factors, such as the training employees required to perform them. The training for a nurse, for example, would be ranked higher than that for a waitress. Numerical scores would be assigned to each factor considered, and these would be added up. If two jobs had the same final score, they would be viewed as "comparable" and so they would pay the same. If an engineer and a violinist were ranked the same, they would receive the same wages.

In this manner, by placing the labor market in the hands of experts and government administrators, women would be spared the injustice of a free market that undervalues their work.

A Call for Revolution

In the '60s, liberal feminists gave the free market a vote of no confidence by insisting that the government pry open doors of opportunity for women. Their solution to this inequity was affirmative action, a policy of reform. Most of these feminists wanted equal representation within a system they considered to be discriminatory; they wanted to reform the system to get their share of the free market pie.

With comparable worth, gender feminists are demanding a radical redistribution of the power and wealth of society. Their solution is revolutionary. If comparable worth were to succeed, it would deliver a death blow to the free market by turning one of its key mechanisms—the labor market—over to government control. As Peter Schwartz declares in *Reason* magazine: "For comparable worth is more than an intervention in the free market—it is a denial of the *possibility* of a free market."[4]

Comparable worth advocates are not reformers who wish to tinker with the system. They aim at nothing less than replacing the free-market system with centralized government control of the economy. The *Wall Street Journal* prophetically hailed one of the early comparable worth programs in these words: "The lid was removed from a Pandora's box and a new approach for setting pay for women has made its escape. Under the innocuous name of 'comparable worth,' it would abolish the labor market and have everyone's pay set by bureaucrats."[5]

In the anthology *Women and the Workplace*, gender feminist Heidi Hartmann sketches the scope of the revolution, of which comparable worth is only one component:

> We must study the subconscious—both how these behavioral rules are internalized and how they grow out of personality structure. At this level, the formation of personality, there have been several attempts to study the production of gender, the *socially* imposed differentiation of humans based on biological sex differences.[6]

Comparable worth is merely a wedge to get at the far larger problem of social and gender justice: "In attacking both patriarchy and capitalism we will have to find ways to change both society-wide institutions and our most deeply ingrained habits. It will be a long, hard struggle."[7] Comparable worth is not an attack on the efficiency of the marketplace; it is an assault on the possibility of economic freedom ever providing justice to women. The free market, it is argued, is irredeemably corrupt. What else can explain the fact that nurses, who save lives, are paid less than garbage men?

A few years ago, gender feminists edged disturbingly close to achieving this goal. Comparable worth became a national issue in 1977 when it was championed by President Carter's administration and duly supported by Eleanor Holmes Norton, then chair of the Equal Employment Opportunity Commission (EEOC).

Under Carter, comparable worth language was scheduled to be included in the sex discrimination guidelines of the programs of the Office of Federal Contract Compliance, the agency that makes sure federal contractors implement affirmative action. But the language did not come into effect during Carter's term, and the ensuing Reagan administration was hostile to comparable worth. The language was cut out.

Disillusioned, advocates of comparable worth turned to the state level and began to wage their war through the legal system. The courts became the vital battleground of comparable worth. If legislation could not get past a hostile Republican administration and an ambivalent Congress, then the courts of the land provided another route.

In 1981 the Supreme Court delivered a landmark decision in *County of Washington v. Gunther*. This case involved female prison guards who claimed they were being paid less than male guards doing equal work. The court's confusing ruling opened the door for plaintiffs to bring suit under Title VII without having to meet the equal work standard.

In 1983 Judge Tanner of the U.S. District Court of the Western District of Washington ruled on *American Federation of State, County and Municipal Employees (AFSCME) v. Washington*. In this case, the union charged that Washington state was allowing the free market to set wages for public employees even though the state had commissioned a series of comparable worth studies. The court ruled that the State of Washington was in violation of Title VII and that it had to implement the studies' findings.

The decision was later overturned. But in the wake of the initial AFSCME decision, state after state authorized comparable worth studies and passed legislation affecting its public workers. On the federal level, attempts to institute comparable worth have been persistent but less successful. Thus far, the private sector has resisted attempts to legislate wage control. It is in the private sector that the battle lines will be drawn.

Is the Free Market Just?

When individualist feminists look at the free market, they see a coordinating mechanism, which functions spontaneously. It not only balances supply with demand, but also expresses the economic self-interest of everyone involved in it. They see a system in which people buy when the price is right and sell for a similar reason.

Gender feminists view the same economic landscape and see a system of class and gender oppression. To them the marketplace is an expression of white male culture and must be destroyed. For gender feminists, the free market cannot be corrected to provide women with justice. For one thing, the oppressing class—white males—will not allow this to occur. Gender justice for women must be wrenched from men. For another thing, the labor market is inherently unjust to women. It must be replaced with a system that expresses the ideal of sexual correctness rather than the imperfect preferences of individuals. It must be placed under centralized government control.

The schism between individualist and gender feminists on this issue is unbridgeable, because the disagreement is ideological and fundamental. Joan Acker clearly presents the gender feminist view:

> Comparable worth takes issue with the theory that wages are set by the unseen hand of the market, or by genderless returns to human capital. These theories are major ideological justifications for the contemporary class structure. Comparable worth has the potential to expose such theories as ideology.[8]

To gender feminists the current labor market is an expression of patriarchal capitalism, which oppresses women as a class. To individualist feminists, the unrestrained free market is an expression of economic freedom and self-ownership. Just as freedom of speech derives from every human being's right to use his or her own body, so freedom of exchange derives from that same inalienable right. In his essay explaining the free market, "The Market System," George Hildebrand comments that "The labor market is a market for labor services, where those services are provided by free human beings who cannot be compelled to supply them for a single instant beyond their willingness to do so."[9]

The price of labor, like the price of anything else, does not embody a collective moral ideal such as social equality; it expresses the individual preferences of buyers and sellers. Sometimes those preferences seem morally wrong. To many, it seems wrong that a football player receives more money than a doctor who is researching AIDS. But consumers obviously value the concrete pleasure of watching a football game more than they value the abstract and (usually) indirect benefits of an AIDS cure. The bottom line is: it is the consumer's hard-earned money to spend as he or she sees fit. Everyone has the right to spend his or her money unwisely.

Gender feminists wish to correct the "wrong" preferences of consumers and employers by yanking choice away from them and compelling them to distribute their money in a proper manner—proper by gender feminist standards, of course. At this point in this process, one begins to wonder whose money it is. A genius whose work is valued by no one will be and should be paid nothing. Only by taking away choice from consumers and employers, only by taking away the right of a human being to vote with his or her own money, can this alleged injustice of the free market be corrected. Again, the key moral point lies in the question Whose money is it? Through their actions, gender feminists claim that the wealth is theirs—or, at least, the government's—to redistribute in a just manner. Joan Acker makes this point clearly:

"Ultimately, comparable worth intends to redistribute money, and perhaps power, from men to women."[10]

The issue is *Who* should have the power? Should individuals—as employers, employees, and consumers—have the power to negotiate and exchange their own labor and property on the free market? Or should the state have the power to override those choices? Gender feminists are well aware that an individual who spends his or her dollar is making a political statement. Acker knows that the battleground of comparable worth is not economic; it is political:

> Pay equity, it was clear from the beginning, was a political question. I use the term politics broadly to stand for contests over power, in this case power to define and power to control the comparable worth project and ultimately the classification and compensation system of the state.[11]

In their anthology *Women and the Workplace*, gender feminists Martha Blaxall and Barbara Reagan present an equally clear picture of this political attack:

> The present status of women in the labor market and the current arrangement of sex-segregated jobs is the result of a long process of interaction between patriarchy and capitalism.... Men will have to be forced to give up their favored positions in the division of labor.[12]

Theories of the Wage Gap

The only shortcut through this ideological maze is to return to one of the fundamental questions that comparable worth claims to be addressing. That question is: Why are women paid less than men?

The stock answer that usually comes back is "because of the wage gap and sex segregation." This answer explains very little, and only prompts another question, namely, Do these things result from discrimination or from some other factor? Is there something that explains the wage gap in terms that have nothing to do with injustice?

Many theories have addressed the wage gap. In her book, *A Matter of Choice: A Critique of Comparable Worth by a Skeptical Feminist*, economist Jennifer Roback offers a compelling argument that marital status is the true determining factor in the wage gap.

> The fact [is] that never-married women earn much more than women who have been married—essentially the same amount as never-married men. This pattern has been observed at least since the 1960s. Controlling for marital status alone closes nearly all of the earnings gap.[13]

Roback asks why the sexes experience marriage so differently. Her answer is:

> Married women tend to have children, and ... most of the responsibility for raising them. This usually entails ... leaving the labor force to care for children, either for a short or long time. This absence from the labor force has important economic consequences that have nothing to do with discrimination.[14]

Roback argues that the wage gap is largely a function of how little time married women have to devote to their careers. Indeed, many women choose less demanding jobs in order to have free time for their families. This, in turn, means that they are less productive on the job and they accumulate less of what is called human capital—that is, occupational training and on-the-job experience. Moreover, married women are more likely to quit their jobs because of family pressures. They are more likely to seek out jobs that allow easy entry and exit.

In short, the wage gap reflects the fact that most women have two careers that compete with each other: home and work. Of the two, home usually wins out. Whether this dilemma is fair—whether men should assume more of the burdens of family life—is an intriguing question, but not one that comparable worth addresses.

In the *Harvard Law Review* of 1986 Paul Weiler supports Roback's theory by noting several factors that explain aspects of the wage gap, among them: men work more hours than women, women stay in jobs for shorter periods, and men's jobs tend to be more hazardous. Once these factors are considered, Weiler maintains that there is a 10 to 15 percent difference between what men and women are paid, rather than the 40 percent usually cited.

Advocates of comparable worth usually ignore any factor other than discrimination. After all, if the wage disparity could be explained away, what would happen to the claim that the market is unjust? And if the wage gap is actually closer to 10 or 15 percent instead of a staggering 40 percent, what would happen to the urgency of their cry for gender justice? Ideologically, gender feminists cannot afford to credit the possibility that many women *choose* to take lower-paying, less demanding jobs.

Even if gender feminists acknowledge that marriage plays a role in the wage gap, this does not change their argument. Marriage and the traditional family are viewed as two more patriarchal institutions oppressing women. These institutions are simply working in tandem with the marketplace to keep women down. In *Women and the Workplace*, Blaxall and Reagan explain that "Low wages keep women dependent on men because they encourage women to marry. Married women must perform domestic chores for their husbands. Men benefit, then, from both higher wages and the domestic division of labor."[15]

There are at least two senses in which blaming the wage gap on capitalism may be justified. First, the marketplace expresses the desires of those who participate in it. The free market may be accurately reflecting the preference of married women who want jobs that leave them time for their families.

Second, the market place spontaneously coordinates supply with demand, and both are determining factors of price. In his essay "Benefits and Costs of Comparable Worth," Mark R. Killingsworth gives an example of how a large wage gap can result entirely from the market phenomenon of demand, with no discrimination at all:

> Suppose a firm employs two kinds of translators: French-English and Spanish-English. Their skill, effort, responsibility and working conditions are the same. Should these two kinds of translators actually receive the same pay, as would presumably be required under a comparable worth law? Perhaps.[16]

Having set up a situation of equal pay for comparable worth, Killingsworth changes merely one factor and phrases the question: "But now suppose the translators are in Montreal. Would we necessarily expect them to be paid the same in this case, even in the absence of discrimination?"[17]

In this situation, the French-English translator would be paid much more because of a greater natural demand for his or her services. Equally, Killingsworth observes that a wage gap can result solely from scarcity.

He uses the time-honored example of comparing apples and oranges and cites a proponent of comparable worth who told a hearing of the U.S. Congress that a nutritional evaluation of the two fruits was both sensible and appealing. The proponent went on to claim that—just as one can evaluate different fruits by assigning points for such characteristics as vitamins, minerals, and proteins, so one can also evaluate jobs by assigning points for such factors as training required and dangers involved.

Killingsworth doubts whether the laws of supply and demand can be so easily circumvented: "But can one really use nutritional evaluations to set prices for apples and oranges?... The first frost in Florida will provide an unambiguously negative answer."[18]

Theories of Sex Segregation

The second explanation offered for the lower wages of women is the existence of sex segregation in the workplace. In other words, women tend to cluster in low-paying jobs, while men occupy the higher-paying and more prestigious ones. Estimates vary, but it is commonly said that 80 percent of working women are in sex segregated jobs, that is, jobs in which women predominate by 70 percent. Examples of sex-segregated workers are nurses and receptionists.

Why has affirmative action not eliminated the pink ghettos? Sylvia Ann Hewlett, in her book *A Lesser Life: The Myth of Women's Liberation in America*, also looks to motherhood as an explanation:

> The *Wall Street Journal* put its finger on the nub of the problem ...: "Aglow with talent and self-confidence, young women who came of age in the early 1970s breezed through college, picked up their law degrees and MBA's and began sprinting up the corporate ladder."[19]

But there was a catch: "These same women found their careers 'sabotaged by motherhood.' Although most of these women chose joyfully to become mothers and would have a hard time seeing their babies as saboteurs, the *Journal* hit the nail on the head."[20]

Much of the explanation of sex segregation lies in the desire many women demonstrate for motherhood. They prefer jobs that leave them time for their families. Not surprisingly, gender feminists Blaxall and Reagan bypass the issue of whether such women choose "lesser" jobs. They offer a different theory, one that casts a much more oppressive light on the situation:

> Occupational segregation of the sexes results from the interaction of a
> well-entrenched and complex set of institutions that perpetuates the
> inferior position of women in the labor market, since all pressures within
> society, be they familial, legal, economic, cultural, or historical, tend to
> reinforce and support occupational segregation.[21]

As with the wage gap, gender feminism's accusation of sex segregation is based upon a complex theory of capitalism. Heidi Hartmann
spells out this theory in her essay, "Capitalism, Patriarchy, and Job Segregation by Sex":

> It is my contention that the roots of women's present social status lie in
> this sex-ordered division of labor.... Not only must the hierarchical nature
> of the division of labor between the sexes be eliminated, but the very
> division of labor between the sexes itself must be eliminated.[22]

With the emergence of capitalism through the Industrial Revolution, the family system was said to be threatened by women and children
who began to enter the labor force freely. Many historians view the migra-
tion of women into the work force as a key to their economic liberation
because women could earn their own money. But gender feminists view
it as a source of economic oppression because men felt threatened and
reacted with a backlash against women's independence. How did men
maintain their superior position in the face of this threat? Blaxall and
Reagan explain:

> By segmenting the labor market and playing workers off against each
> other.... Job segregation by sex is the primary mechanism in capitalist
> society that maintains the superiority of men over women, because it
> enforces lower wages for women in the labor market.[23]

The refusal to consider choice as a factor in the wage gap or sex
segregation comes from such ideological assumptions, which form the
foundation for the policy of comparable worth.

Just Price and Inherent Worth

Perhaps the most fundamental assumption of comparable worth is that
of a just price. In his essay, "The Market System," free-market advocate
George H. Hildebrand explains what is meant by this term: "(1) that
'fair' wages and prices have objective meaning in the real world; (2) that
they can be found empirically by appropriate methods; and (3) that they

should be imposed throughout the economy as an act of fundamental social justice."[24]

Just price, as embodied in comparable worth, is the notion that there is a just wage attached to every category of labor. In order to be just, of course, the wage must be independent of the free market, which is inherently oppressive to women. This is to say, the wage must be independent from what anyone would be willing to pay for labor in a system of competition.

As a concept, "just price," or "inherent value," is nothing new. It dates back to the medieval guilds, which determined and legally enforced a so-called just price for their goods. This enabled them to shut out competition and to maximize their profits.

More recently, Karl Marx postulated a labor theory of value, by which goods had inherent worth based on the labor that resided within them. In short, something was worth the time it took to make it. If workers received less pay than the labor theory of value indicated they should, then the workers were being robbed. The extra value was being stolen by the capitalist who had invested none of his or her time in producing the goods.

Comparable worth advocates define a just wage according to a gender theory of value, that is, are women and men compensated comparably? If they are not and if women receive less, then the difference is being stolen from women by men. Gender feminists want to replace the subjective and unjust marketplace with the allegedly objective and fair evaluation of experts, which will be imposed by government bureaucracy.

A problem immediately arises, the same one that confronts socialist planners trying to set prices for goods without reference to supply and demand. Those who administer comparable worth programs find themselves falling back upon the unjust market price of labor as the only guideline that works. The very act of forcing women's wages upward to match those of men relies on market prices, if only because the wages for men have been set by the marketplace. Thus, the results of a free-market process are used as the standard, while all aspects of the marketplace itself are denounced as corrupt.

Over and over, advocates of comparable worth stumble on market prices and market mechanisms. As a personnel administrator involved in implementing comparable worth for the city of San Jose, David Armstrong worried about scarcity: "What do you do with those jobs that are up above the job evaluation average line, so to speak?... Jobs that are critical to operating, say for instance, a city? You can't *drop* them. It looks to me like you still have to pay the market rate."[25]

Comparable Worth: A Growth Industry

In their attempt to avoid the free market, comparable worth advocates have created a boom industry in America. A flood of consulting firms with teams of experts now classifies jobs according to a variable number of factors, usually including skill, mental demands, responsibility, and working conditions. Each category is scored. All categories are added up to arrive at a final score for every type of employment. Thus, seemingly disparate jobs can be compared.

This method has the semblance of objectivity because it uses mathematics and resembles statistics. But critics observe that the process of selecting and weighing the factors is far from objective or scientific. It relies on the very human and subjective judgments of the evaluators. Even the definition of terms is subjective. For example, what constitutes a skill? What definition of worth is being used? The very attempt to measure value requires a standard of value, which is necessarily subjective, and raises questions such as, Of value to whom? and For what?

Even if the problems of definition could be overcome, there is another hurdle. Experts on comparable worth constantly disagree. For example, in Minnesota a registered nurse, a chemist, and a social worker were found to have jobs of equal value, which would be paid the same. Iowa, however, paid a nurse 29 percent more than a chemist.

There can be many reasons for such disagreement. For example, those choosing and paying the experts and analysts can greatly influence the results reached. Moreover, since comparable worth advocates tend to be college-educated and middle-class people, skeptics point to an elitist bias in most of the evaluations. Feminist Brigette Berger has called comparable worth, "one of the more aggressively elitist visions of modern life that has surfaced in recent decades." It is considered elitist because comparable worth stresses factors such as formal education rather than productivity on the job, which inevitably lowers the prestige and compensation of blue-collar workers. Ironically, these are the workers the policy is meant to protect. One of the women interviewed by Joan Acker for her book, *Doing Comparable Worth*, poignantly complains about the effect of comparable worth on workers' morale in her place of employment:

> I think [job evaluation] is terrible. I mean, it's accepting the basic premises of inequality. And no matter what way you say it, you end up saying, "Isn't it true that a clerical worker is better ... than a garbage man?" ... you're really saying, "Who is worth more?"[26]

For those who feel they have been evaluated unfairly, there is little recourse. The evaluators control the content, the application, and the technology of the system they are implementing. The isolation surrounding this process veils the fact that it is biased and subjective. In his influential anthology, *Comparable Worth: Issues and Alternatives*, editor E. Robert Livernash admits "there is simply no known technique by which job 'worth' in any intrinsic sense can be measured."[27] Livernash continues: "From a logical basis, it is impossible to prove that a set of given structural wage or salary relationships are or are not discriminatory. Absent specific evidence showing employer intent, there is no universally accepted value system."[28]

Conclusion

Comparable worth does not and cannot work. It violates the most basic of economic truths: scarcity determines the price and supply of a commodity. It also disregards traditional measures of worth, such as seniority, merit, and character. Comparable worth is a counterproductive and blatantly unfair policy for both women and men.

Yet fairness is precisely what comparable worth—through the grace of government—promises to deliver. How can government perform this feat? Even pushing aside gender feminism's accusation that the state is a male weapon of oppression, government cannot impose measures that society is not already willing to accept. Government—if it is representative—is a reflection of society, even as the free market is. Both are created by the individual preferences of society. The free market is shaped by how we spend our money, government by how we cast our votes.

The relevant difference between the two institutions is that the free market has no way to make anyone buy or sell something while the government can regulate our behavior through the force of law. In terms of the workplace, the free market cannot institutionalize an injustice, such as discrimination. Indeed, throughout history, the free market has opened up opportunities for workers—regardless of race, sex, or religion—while government has traditionally protected the status quo.

In South Africa, for example, government policies have discriminated against blacks far more than the marketplace has. For example, despite legislation that prohibited blacks from holding certain jobs, black laborers flocked to wherever there were good jobs. Despite government penalties against hiring blacks for certain jobs, employers violated the law to obtain cheap labor. Government regulations can never change the economic truth of supply and demand. All that the state can do is to make this principle operate underground.

In short, government discriminates more than the free market, simply because employers who discriminate must bear the cost of doing so. They limit the pool of talent from which they can draw; they lose good employees to companies who treat them better; they lose customers who disapprove of discrimination; they endanger their reputations in the community. In his pivotal work, *The Economics of Discrimination*, Gary Becker demonstrates that discrimination reduces the income of those who discriminate *as well as* the income of the victims. Thus, the free market tends to be self-correcting. The profit motive is an argument against discrimination.

Politicians have no comparable incentive. And their track record on tinkering with the free market to benefit minorities and women has been dismal. Robert Livernash comments on one such social experiment, the minimum wage laws:

> Economists have already produced quantities of evidence to demonstrate how the minimum wage has deprived the young and the unskilled workers of jobs, with consequent extremely high unemployment rates. Under the comparable worth proposal, the equivalent of the minimum wage would be imposed.[29]

George H. Hildebrand sketches the probable consequences of comparable worth: "(1) unemployment rates for females will rise, (2) unemployment of females also will rise, (3) the major victims will be the poorest female workers, (4) welfare dependency will grow, (5) female youngsters will be large losers of job opportunities."[30]

Ironically, gender feminists are also growing cynical about whether comparable worth will better the lot of women. Joan Acker served as a member of the Oregon Comparable Worth Task Force, established in 1983. After a great deal of frustration with the bureaucracy, she began to ask such questions as: How do you know when the goal has been achieved? Has pay equity really upset old patterns of inequity? When she (and other feminists) actively tried to remedy sex bias within the evaluation system itself, they encountered a brick wall of opposition. From this, Acker concludes that "Attempts to minimize sex bias will be met with powerful opposition.... The elimination of sex bias is potentially subversive of existing hierarchies ... in the long run, it would seem that the elimination of sex bias depends on an overall attack on inequality."[31]

Acker began to suspect that pay equity programs were intentionally complex and inaccessible in order to disguise gender bias. For example, evaluation systems often did not acknowledge the talents that characterized women's work. One study developed by the U.S. Department of Labor did not consider taking care of children—as performed by day care workers—to be a skill. It was simply part of being a woman. After serving on the Comparable Worth Task Force, Acker concludes that "Feminists' acceptance of job comparison has allowed the state to control and manage the issue without the kind of fundamental change we know is necessary. At the same time, it allows the state to argue that they have given us what we wanted."[32]

A growing number of gender feminists seem to realize that comparable worth cannot work. Absent from this dawning awareness, however, is any willingness to question the ideology that has led women down blind alleys. Equal pay did not work; affirmative action failed; comparable worth is not delivering. But gender feminism remains dogmatically convinced that the free market is the enemy of women and that government control is the solution.

I shudder to think what economic policy may be next.

Notes

1. *Chapter 75*, First Extraordinary Session, Laws of 1983.
2. Sara M. Evans and Barbara J. Nelson, eds., *Wage Justice: Comparable Worth and the Paradox of Technocratic Reform* (Chicago: University of Chicago Press, 1989), p. ix.
3. Joan Acker, *Doing Comparable Worth: Gender, Class, and Pay Equity* (Philadelphia: Temple University, 1989), p. 5.
4. Peter Schwartz, "Women's Worth: Is Comparable Worth Good for Women?" *Reason*, July 1982, p. 40.
5. *Wall Street Journal*, July 16, 1981.
6. Heidi Hartmann, "Capitalism, Patriarchy and Job Segregation by Sex," in *Women and the Workplace: The Implications of Occupational Segregation*, ed. Martha Blaxall and Barbara Reagan (Chicago: University of Chicago Press, 1976), p. 169.
7. Ibid.
8. Acker, *Doing Comparable Worth*, p. 22.
9. George Hildebrand, "The Market System" in *Comparable Worth: Issues and Alternatives*, ed. E. Robert Livernash (Washington D.C.: Equal Employment Advisory Council, 1984), p. 85.
10. Acker, *Doing Comparable Worth*, p. 21.
11. Ibid., p. 57.
12. Blaxall and Reagan, *Women and the Workplace*, p. 168.
13. Jennifer Roback, *A Matter of Choice: A Critique of Comparable Worth by a Skeptical Feminist* (New York: Priority Press, 1986), p. 30.
14. Ibid.
15. Blaxall and Reagan, *Women and the Workplace*, p. 139.
16. Mark R. Killingsworth, "Benefits and Costs of Comparable Worth," in *Pay*

Equity: Means and Ends, ed. Michael G. Abbott (Kingston, Ontario: John Deutsch Institute, 1990), p. 49.

17. Ibid.

18. Ibid., p. 50.

19. Sylvia Ann Hewlett, *A Lesser Life: The Myth of Women's Liberation in America* (New York: William Morrow, 1986), p. 15.

20. Ibid.

21. Blaxall and Reagan, *Women and the Workplace*, p. 2.

22. Blaxall and Reagan, *Women and the Workplace*, pp. 137–138.

23. Blaxall and Reagan, *Women in the Workplace*, p. 139.

24. Hildebrand, "Market System," p. 83.

25. Frances C. Hutner, *Equal Pay for Comparable Worth: The Working Woman's Issue of the Eighties* (New York: Praeger, 1986), p. 76.

26. Acker, *Doing Comparable Worth*, p. 85.

27. Livernash, *Comparable Worth*, p. 3.

28. Ibid., p. 10.

29. Ibid., p. 84.

30. Hildebrand, "Market System," p. 106.

31. Acker, *Doing Comparable Worth*, p. 189.

32. Ibid., p. 100.

CHAPTER EIGHT

Marriage and the Family
An Ideological Battleground

To the sexually correct feminist, marriage oppresses women and the family breeds patriarchy. Both result from capitalism. Happily married women are considered pathological and traitorous. To justify this blast of enmity, gender feminists point to the soaring rate of domestic violence even though violence against women—as measured by the murder rate—has not increased except in proportion to population growth. Although the gender feminist view of marriage borders on the absurd—e.g., housework as "surplus value"—it is key to understanding the depth of hatred they aim at heterosexual sex and men. This, in turn, is crucial to understanding the emotions underlying sexual correctness.

What Is the Family?
The Conservative and the Gender View

Conservatives believe that the traditional family is the basic building block of society's institutions; it weaves the very fabric of cultural values. Gender feminists agree. Beyond this threshold of agreement, however, an ideological brawl has broken out between these two opposing voices over the institutions of marriage and the family.

On their side of the divide, conservatives champion the family as indispensable to civilization. Only families can offer the long-term emotional stability and commitment child rearing requires. Only families can ensure reproduction and the proper socialization of children. Beyond this, families provide an emotional and sexual support system for married couples, who need a shelter against the buffets of a hostile world.

Without the family, conservatives predict the breakdown of moral values and an upsurge of social anarchy.

From the opposite end of the political spectrum, gender feminists roundly reject the family for much the same reasons that conservatives embrace it. It is a bastion of traditional values and a training ground for society's institutions. In short, the family is the foundation of patriarchal capitalism, which gender feminists claim is *the* source of women's oppression.

The conflict over the American family is further complicated by how quickly this institution is redefining itself. In the 1950s, the typical family consisted of a husband and a wife, with two or three children. The wife stayed at home while the husband worked outside the home to provide for his family. Today, there seems to be no typical family, no typical nuclear unit. Divorced parents, unwed mothers, and adopting homosexuals have changed the picture of parenthood. Domestic life has been transformed by economic realities that force most mothers into the workplace and out of the home.

In her essay, "The Changing Role of the Family," Laura Levin explains:

> In 1950 only 18% of wives with children under eighteen were employed. By 1980 that figure had risen to 54%.... While our traditional stereotype of the American Family has included an employed father and an unemployed mother ... now only 12% of American households fit that model.[1]

This transformation of the family presents something of a problem for gender feminists. It is difficult to consider something that takes as many forms as the modern family to be uniformly unjust in every instance. Yet gender feminists see a common denominator within all marriages, namely, the oppression of its female members.

This is true even of a family that consists entirely of females, a family with only a single mother and a daughter, for example. This type of family is oppressed by men because its interactions are a reflection of the injustice of patriarchy that both females encounter in the workplace and the political system. Because they are females, their family unit will be economically poorer and have fewer opportunities than a comparable family unit that is male, such as a man and his son.

The fight over the family and marriage is an ideological one. When conservatives and gender feminists view the same institutions, they draw dramatically different conclusions. Conservatives see a natural and smoothly functioning unit, whose negative characteristics—such as domestic violence—are aberrations. Gender feminists look at families and see *Diary of a Mad Housewife*—a novel of the late 1960s by Sue Kaufman, who chronicled the angst of an upper middle-class urban housewife. Abuses, such as domestic violence, are considered to be unfiltered expressions of the married state.

Feminist Views of Marriage and the Family

Within feminism the discussion of marriage has shifted over the past few decades. Virtually all feminists share a belief that men and women experience the family in totally different ways. This is not a biological truism; it is a statement of political and economic fact. For centuries marriage laws favored men to such a degree that a wife could often be involuntarily committed to a mental institution on her husband's signature. Even after marriage laws had been reformed, the institution itself seemed to favor men, for example, in the distribution of housework.

But liberal feminists view marriage as salvageable, as an institution that needs reform rather than elimination. The liberal feminist critique of the family began in the '60s, with Betty Friedan's pivotal work *The Feminine Mystique* (1963). Friedan argued that American women of that era were enslaved by domesticity and defined by their roles as mother and wife. Although she called the family a "comfortable concentration camp," Friedan's goal was not to eliminate marriage. She merely wanted women to insist on more from life, for them to reach outside of marriage for fulfillment.

Years later, when some feminists used Friedan's theories to argue for abolishing the family, however, she wrote a second work, *The Second Stage* (1981). Here, she explained that her theories had been misunderstood. Gender feminists were taking her criticisms much farther than she had intended them to go. Friedan asked for a reconsideration of marriage. She pleaded for feminists to move away from antifamily rhetoric and back to a dialogue addressing the needs of most women, who were wives and mothers. She called for a humanistic evolution that would enrich the institution of the family by including the needs and desires of men in the picture. Betty Friedan represents the liberal feminist point of view.

Interestingly, another pioneer in woman's liberation has also felt the need to publish a second book to defend the concept of family, namely, Germaine Greer. In the '70s, Greer, with her outrageous behavior and shocking language, declared a guerrilla war against dependency on men.

Greer called for the revolutionary breakdown of sex roles. She encouraged women to be promiscuous and otherwise sexually adventurous. She claimed that women have no idea of how much men hate them. Greer recounted stories of gang rape and brutality and seemed to consider such violence to be the norm between men and women. Her solution: women should refuse to marry. If they do marry, they should refuse to be monogamous or to accept the "trappings" of marriage such as the husband's last name, a shared tax return, a wedding ring. Equally, women should reject their role as consumers in a capitalist society.

Despite this gender rhetoric, however, Greer was not clear in her condemnation of the family. Nor was she unsympathetic to men, whom she considered to be fellow victims of the system. Instead, Greer wanted to replace the status quo with what she called an "organic family." In a later book, however, Greer forthrightly defends a more traditional version of the family. She accepts the idea that husband, wife, and children constitute the basic familial unit.

The liberal ideal of an equal marriage in which men and women equally share responsibilities, including housework, has been dismissed by gender feminists. In her essay "The Many Faces of Backlash," Florence Rush jettisons the concept of human liberation on the grounds that male liberation has no historical basis. Rush considers liberals who espouse such ideals to be traitors. Their support "is deceptive and far more insidious, and has taken an enormous toll. Many women find it hard to resist the promise of a caring, equal relationship with a sympathetic man."[2]

The truly radical assault on the family began with Kate Millett's book *Sexual Politics* (1970). Although Millett's views were extreme, she presented them in a dispassionate and well-researched manner that lent her credibility. In dealing with male/female relations ("sexual politics"), Millett dwelt almost obsessively on pornography and sado-masochistic literature, rather than on love, motherhood, or successful marriages. To her, pornography seemed to epitomize the male/female relationship. And in attacking sexual politics, Millett attacked the entire structure of power in society that is, patriarchy. Marriage was *the* agency that maintained the traditional pattern of man's power over woman.

Millett's theories were followed up and fleshed out by such extreme voices as Shulamith Firestone, Susan Brownmiller, and Ti Atkinson. As the edifice of gender ideology was constructed, it began to have an impact on the mainstream of feminism. Gender feminist Catharine MacKinnon described the shift from liberalism to the antimarriage point of view. This was a change from desiring equality to demanding equity:

> Then [after liberal feminism], there was a women's movement that criticized
> ... war as male ejaculation. It criticized marriage and the family as institutional

crucibles of male privilege.... Some criticized sex, including the institution of intercourse, as a strategy and practice in subordination.[3]

The titles of popular feminist books from the early movement underscore the schism between gender feminists and women who choose domesticity. A partial list includes Jill Johnston's *Lesbian Nation* (1973), which called heterosexual females traitors; Kate Millett's *Sexual Politics* (1970), which redefined heterosexual sex as a power struggle; Kathrin Perutz's *Marriage Is Hell* (1972); and Ellen Peck's *The Baby Trap* (1971), which argued that babies block liberation. The ideological message was clear: the personal is political; marriage is legalized prostitution; heterosexual intercourse is rape; men are the enemy; families are prisons.

When domesticity was not being torn to political shreds, it was ignored. For example, the popular anthology *Sisterhood Is Powerful* contains seventy-four essays. Only one had anything to do with motherhood. Apparently this was not an issue that concerns women.

Background of Gender Feminism's Analysis of Marriage

Gender feminist Catharine MacKinnon describes the shift from the liberal view of marriage, family, and heterosexual sex: Gender feminists' scorn for marriage and the family has not only distanced them from liberals, but from the majority of women who have chosen marriage and motherhood.

What are the specifics of gender feminism's theory of marriage? Gender feminists consider marriage to be an involuntary state, in which women have the status of chattel. To them, marriage and the family are inextricably bound up with private property, the class structure, and the mode of production. In other words, the family is an aspect of capitalism. Much of this analysis rests on Marxist theory, especially on the work of Friedrich Engels, co-author of the *Communist Manifesto*.

He argued that the oppression of women sprang from the nuclear family. But Engels—much quoted by Kate Millett, a pioneer of gender theory—was contemptuous of the notion that the family had subordinated women throughout history. Instead he placed the blame firmly on the shoulders of capitalism, which had destroyed the prestige of women within the family. Engels wrote, "That woman was the slave of man at the commencement of society is one of the most absurd notions ... Women were not only free, but they held a highly respected position in the early stages of civilization and were the great power among the clans."[4]

Thus, gender feminists romanticize preindustrial times. On the family farm, it is claimed, men's and women's work was equal. Although critics might question whether eighteenth-century men really did more cooking, cleaning, or diaper-changing than their twentieth-century descendants, gender feminists insist that the prestige of women's work used to equal that of men's.

In the nineteenth century, it is claimed, industrialization brought a "separation between home and productive work"[5] and caused a transfer of men's labor from the home to the factory, while women remained at the hearth. Men came to dominate the public realm, women the private. Women accepted such an unfavorable arrangement—including monogamy—because it offered security from the growing complexity of life. Susan Brownmiller later even claimed it offered safety from rape by other men.

Thus, in this view, the nuclear family did not evolve as a matter of biology but as a result of industrialization. In other words, men left the home to become wage earners, and consequently women assumed the care of the family within the home. Women's labor became an essential but subordinate aspect of freeing men to earn a wage.

Gender feminists cannot ignore the blatant fact that industrialization offered women an unprecedented opportunity to earn wages outside the home, that is, to be economically independent. But, they argue, such freedom was illusory. Women were paid low wages and shut out of many jobs. Under capitalism, they argue, women assumed the role of breeders, housewives, and buyers of consumer goods. Women maintained the workforce by providing laundry, food, and cleaning services for men, all without pay. Moreover, mothers provided the next generation of laborers for capitalist exploitation, complete with the appropriate socialization.

Karl Marx claimed, "The reproduction of the working class implies at the same time the transmission and accumulation of skills from one generation to another."[6] In their pamphlet, *Counter-Planning from the Kitchen: Wages for Housework*, Nicole Cox and Silvia Federici explain the benefits provided to capitalism by mothers and housewives. They argue that such domesticated women perpetuate the cycle of capitalism: "Housework ... is servicing the wage earner physically, emotionally, sexually, getting him ready to work day after day for the wage. It is taking care of our children ... and ensuring that they too perform in ways expected of them under capitalism."[7]

But gender feminists had a problem with Engels and Marx, who assumed that men *as a sex* had no stake in exerting power over women. In other words, they rejected gender as the basis of class analysis. The important factor in class analysis was one's relationship to the mode of production, that is, whether one was a worker or a capitalist. Marx believed that, once they entered the workforce, women would became the equals of men. In other words, Engels and Marx denied that women, as a sex, formed a class with unique interests and needs.

To explain that women have gender interests distinct from and opposed to those of men, gender feminists had to reach beyond Marxism. They evolved a theory of patriarchy, of *male* capitalism, in which women were oppressed as much by male culture as by the economic system. These twin evils supported each other on the collective back of women.

As for the women who wanted to become housewives, gender feminists made no effort to woo them toward a more liberated view, quite the contrary. Such women were insulted as "sexual spittoons" and their attachment to their families was seen as a sign of pathology. In her essay *Taking Our Eyes Off the Guys*, Sonia Johnson explained the reasoning behind such shock tactics: "Women have been seasoned as slaves and prostitutes.... But no matter how we're seasoned—as prostitute or as wife, which is the same thing—we're seasoned in the patriarchal family almost exclusively to serve sexual functions."[8]

These opinions were backed up with action. For example, the Women's International Terrorist Conspiracy from Hell (WITCH) disrupted a 1969 fashion show for brides by chanting to the tune of the Wedding March: "Here come the slaves/Off to their graves."

Gender feminism's view of the family has divided women into hostile camps. Most women—however much they might want to reform marriage—do not want to abolish their husbands and children. Yet gender feminists seem to demand nothing less.

When dealing with the protestations of women who wanted to be wives and mothers, gender feminist groups, such as the Southern Women's Writing Collective, treated them as conditioned, like Pavlovian dogs, by male culture. In short, they could be retrained. In a joint essay, "Sex Resistance in Heterosexual Arrangements," the Writing Collective expressed both its militant inflexibility and its disregard for "domesticated" women: "The desires that were socially incarnated in us in order to effect our subordination to men can be named and disowned. After all, if we can teach pigeons to play ping-pong ... perhaps we can teach ourselves to prefer a nonsexualized woman–identification."[9]

Recently, gender feminists have been edging away from outright condemnations of marriage and the family. Perhaps they perceive how unpopular this stand makes them among the majority of women. In the face of such a backlash, gender feminists have become more subdued in their statements about marriage and motherhood. But the goal remains the same: a revolution to sweep away patriarchy.

The Conflict Over Housework

The conflict between gender and liberal feminists can be illustrated through the issue of housework. Both ideologies begin by assuming that there is something inherently oppressive about housework. Beyond this point, agreement breaks down.

Liberals generally view housework as a problem in the division of labor. That is, they see an imbalance in the amount of domestic chores performed by women as opposed to those performed by men. The solutions offered by liberals are often individual and private, rather than public or political. For example, couples are encouraged to work out schedules that divide the labor more fairly. Men are encouraged to share the load equally.

Gender feminists take a more extreme stance. First of all, housework is not viewed as an imbalance to be corrected. It is a direct expression of man's oppression of woman, which cannot be reformed by a schedule but must be swept away. Men cannot be convinced to assume their fair share, because such fairness goes against their class interests. In her essay "The Dynamics of Marriage and Motherhood," Beverly Jones outlines this conflict, which can have no individual or personal solutions. Jones finds that

> A relationship between a man and a woman is no more or less personal a relationship than ... a master and his slave, a teacher and his student. Of course, there are personal, individual qualities to a particular relationship ... but they are so overshadowed by the class nature of the relationship.[10]

As for the beneficiary of housework, gender feminists are clear: men as a class and capitalism as a system are the beneficiaries. Thus, there are two layers of exploitation, men and capitalism, which combine to form patriarchy. Gender feminists explain the benefits of housework to capitalism. Capitalism is the process by which those who own the means of production pay wages to workers who produce goods worth more than the wages they are paid. This "excess" is called the surplus value of labor, and it is absorbed by capitalists as profit.

Where does the housewife fit in? According to gender feminists such as Dallas Costa, housework also produces a surplus value that is absorbed by capitalism.[11] The surplus value of housework is that it enables men's labor. The fact that individual men sometimes perform domestic work does not alter this scenario, because men—as a class—do not share the economic dependence of women.

Housework is said to have a direct impact on the wages and job opportunities offered to women in the workplace. Because of the precedent of housework, employers can pay women less than they are worth. Moreover, by encouraging women to stay at home, men can reduce the competition for money and power. Gender feminist Del Martin explained this latter benefit to men as follows:

> If society succeeds in pressuring women to remain home, the labor market is cut in half, and competition for jobs, money, and power is thereby cut in half. Capitalism thrives on competition, but when too many qualified competitors go after the same goal, the system begins to get clogged up.[12]

Exactly how capitalism can benefit from restricting the pool of labor and talent from which it can draw is not fully explained. Indeed, an excess of qualified workers undercutting each other would seem—by gender feminism's standards—to be a capitalistic dream.

Nevertheless, Del Martin's analysis of housework does illustrate an important connection within gender feminist theory. Martin's comments are one aspect of her book entitled *Battered Wives*. For gender feminists, housework and wife assault are two points on the same continuum of woman's oppression.

Domestic Violence: The Naked Face of Patriarchy

> Patriarchy requires violence or the subliminal threat of violence in order to maintain itself.... The most dangerous situation for a woman is not an unknown man in the street, or even the enemy in wartime, but a husband or lover in the isolation of their own home. —Gloria Steinem[13]

In the last few years, the issue of domestic violence has stirred up a furor of concern among women of all ages and ideologies. Domestic violence is particularly frightening because it occurs where women are supposed to safe—when they are at home behind locked doors and shielded from strangers. Yet statistics indicate that women are more likely to be assaulted by a loved one than by a stranger and that domestic assault usually is more violent than street attacks. For women, domestic violence reconfirms a fear that borders on paranoia: the fear that they are safe nowhere and from no one.

In general, three major approaches underlie current discussions of domestic violence, the first two of which tend to come from liberal feminists:

(1) a sociocultural approach that examines the reasons why aggression against women is tolerated by our society; and, (2) a psychological approach that examines the emotional reasons why men are abusive and why women accept it.

The third approach, the one favored by gender feminists, takes an entirely political view and is (3) a class analysis approach, by which men are said to beat women to retain their place in the patriarchal power structure.

In her book, *Heroes of Their Own Lives*, Linda Gordon expresses the gist of gender feminism's analysis:

> The basis of wife-beating is male dominance—not superior physical strength or violent temperament ... but social, economic, political, and psychological power.... Wife-beating is the chronic battering of a person of inferior power who for that reason cannot effectively resist.[14]

There can be no argument: domestic violence is a crime that demands the attention of every feminist. Every woman has the absolute right not to be beaten. But there are at least two major problems with the gender feminist position on domestic violence.

First, gender feminists consider wife assault to be a socioeconomic crime that must be confronted in the political arena. Since domestic violence is viewed as the clash of two antagonistic classes—men and women—individual solutions are dismissed or downplayed as ineffective. These dismissed solutions include, for example, teaching women the art of self-defense and the use of fire arms. But in considering men as a class to be guilty of domestic violence, gender feminists ignore the fact that most men do *not* beat their wives. Whatever statistics are accepted, all of them agree that fewer than 50 percent of husbands beat their wives. Thus, statistics show that men, as a class, are not wife-beaters. Domestic violence actually *is* the aberration that conservatives claim it to be.

Such a conclusion, however, would not further the cause of a socioeconomic revolution. Instead, gender feminists attempt to fuel a gender war that feeds the fears of women.

Second, gender feminists are grafting the issue of domestic violence onto their own political agenda, the pain of battered women is being used to further political goals. Across the nation, women are marching to "take back the night," to end violence against women. On almost every campus, an increasing number of female students report a growing concern about being attacked. It is difficult to remember a time when women felt more threatened by men.

Is this fear justified? Statistics are being bandied about with wild abandon: one in four women will be raped; between 80 and 90 percent of women have been sexually harassed at work; 12 percent of women have experienced sexual abuse during childhood. Many of these statistics and studies contradict each other. Studies that do not conform to the politically/sexually correct position on rape or domestic violence tend to be buried. The "proper" studies are loudly discussed by those who have a vested interest in their findings. Few of these advocates cite their sources, and even fewer critically investigate the studies by asking, for example, how the researchers defined their terms. One reporter who asked this question discovered that purely verbal "lovers' quarrels" were considered sexual abuse.

All of this raises the question of whether these statistics are believable. For example, *Maclean's* magazine—Canada's version of *Time*—recently ran a story entitled "Women in Fear," which purported to chronicle men's reign of terror over women. With rare honesty, the article admitted that it was drawing broad conclusions from a "handful of official records and credible estimates."[15]

Maclean's also reported that "the number of women being killed—234 in Canada in 1990—has grown in recent decades roughly in line with the population increase.... What is different is that women are vocally insisting, with great determination and growing political force, that the carnage end."

In his column entitled "Media Watch," George Bain pointed to statistics on homicides of females in Canada: "Female homicide victims in Canada went from 208 in 1980 to 253 in 1985, and down to 234 in 1990, precisely in lockstep with the number of male homicides, for which the comparable figures were 385, 451 and 422."[16]

From this Bain drew two conclusions: (1) in the last decades murder rates in general rose and then fell; and (2) the figures reflect a widespread problem with violence in society, unrelated to gender.

American statistics agree. According to the latest National Crime Victimization Survey, conducted by the U.S. Bureau of Justice Statistics, sexual assaults on women declined by 20 percent from 1992 to 1993. The leading researchers on domestic violence—Richard J. Gelles and Murray A. Straus—also agree. In two national surveys they found that women were as likely to engage in domestic violence as men. Their 1985 Second National Family Violence Survey also found that a significant decrease in domestic violence had occurred between 1975 and 1985.[17]

In other words, violence against women—as measured by the murder rate—has not increased except in proportion to population growth.

What has increased is the willingness of women to report and protest against such violence. Yet anyone who suggests that domestic violence may be no worse today than it has been for decades is met by howls of outrage from gender feminists, who have a political investment in presenting women as in a state of crisis.

The New Feminist Jurisprudence

The Violence Against Women Act (VAWA), which Congress approved last year as part of the Omnibus Crime Act, advances the gender feminist goal of redistributing power from the ruling class (men) to the oppressed class (women). VAWA defines gender-motivated crimes as federal civil-rights violations, thus converting domestic violence into a hate crime. Under these circumstances, the law recognizes men and women as antagonistic classes to be governed by different standards of law.

The success of the so-called battered-woman syndrome as a defense in murder cases also illustrates how standards of justice have been warped by the politicization of violence against women. Gender feminist Lenore Walker—director of the Domestic Violence Institute—has been instrumental in promoting the battered-woman syndrome. Her ideology is clear:

> A feminist political gender analysis has reframed the problem of violence against women as one of misuse of power by men who have been socialized into believing they have the right to control the women in their lives, even through violent means.[18]

Walker defines what constitutes a battered woman: "A battered woman is a woman who is repeatedly subjected to any forceful physical or psychological behavior by a man in order to coerce her to do something he wants."[19] Even without physical violence, a woman can be deemed battered if, for example, her husband neglects her in favor of work.[20]

Walker's view of women as helpless victims who can be devastated by such abuses as neglect is being translated into legal precedents. Walker argues that battered wives become so demoralized that they lose the capacity to leave the abusive marriage. When such a wife strikes out at her husband, the violence is considered to be self-defense. This is true even if the wife has never been physically threatened or harmed and even if she uses deadly force.

Traditionally, the self-defense plea required that the accused was in "clear and present danger." Now Walker claims that physical danger is not necessary for women to avail themselves of this defense. The battered-woman syndrome appeared as a defense in murder cases in the late 1970s, and has since gained in acceptance. In Canada, the battered woman defense was originally introduced as a means of reducing a charge from murder to manslaughter. It has been extended to obtain complete acquittals even in cases where the man had no history of physical violence.

Similar court cases are beginning to occur in the United States. In 1987, for example, Marlene Wagshall shot her sleeping husband in a fit of jealousy. He survived, after surgery which removed large parts of his stomach, liver and upper intestine. Elizabeth Holtzman, a feminist district attorney for Brooklyn, New York, had the charge reduced from attempted murder to second-degree assault on Wagshall's uncorroborated claim of prior battery. She served one day in jail, with five years probation.[21]

Solution: State Control of the Private Realm

During the last two decades, the slogan "The personal is political" has been edging out in popularity the former feminist touchstone of "a woman's body, a woman's right." After all, if gender feminists are correct, then the choices a woman makes with her own body concern not only herself but impact also on all women as a class. Women as a class have a right to participate in her decisions. Indeed, it could be argued that women do not truly have individual decisions or private interests, they only have interests as a class.

Gender feminist Susan Moller Okin explains this point in her book, *Justice, Gender, and the Family*. Referring to the slogan "The personal is political" as "the central message of feminist critiques" of claims to privacy, she elaborates that "The earliest claims that the personal is political came from those gender feminists of the 1960s and 1970s who argued that, since the family was at the root of women's oppression, it must be 'smashed.'"[22] Okin argues that the family, the so-called personal sphere, must be opened to political change, by force if necessary. The state should reach into the home to make it just:

> Contemporary feminism poses a significant challenge to the long-standing and still-surviving assumption of political theories that the sphere of family and personal life is sharply distinct from the rest of social and political life, that the state can and should restrain itself from intrusion into the domestic scene.[23]

To those who object to state control of the family, Okin replies that the state already intervenes in that it establishes the social background for the functioning of the family. Expanding the intervention, for example, by requiring payment for housework, is a difference of degree, not of kind.

But what about couples who wish to maintain a more traditional marriage? What of those women who want to work out the terms of their family structure for themselves with their husbands? Okin argues that such personal desires are irrelevant; the family is too important a social institution to be abandoned to the arbitrary wishes of the individuals involved.

The terms on which a family divides up housekeeping may seem to be the business of the individuals involved, but in reality it is a matter of social justice. The state must dictate the terms of family life to ensure equity. Okin's specific recommendations for making families just would require nothing less than a total restructuring of the economy. For example, with reference to providing a salary for housewives, Okin suggests that both spouses should have a legal entitlement to every cent coming into the house: "The clearest and simplest way of doing this would be to have employers make out wage checks equally divided between the earner and the partner who provides all or most of his or her unpaid domestic services."[24]

This demand is the logical and inevitable extension of the principle, "The personal is political."

The Personal Is Personal: Individualist Feminism

Fortunately, another tradition within feminism is more suspicious of the state than Okin—individualist feminism. Even the liberal tradition has offered resistance to following the principle of the personal being political to its logical conclusion. In her book, *In Women's Interest*, Lisa S. Price offers some sanity: "The state is interested in control and legitimacy. Feminism is interested in the liberation of women. These interests do not intersect and are in fact fundamentally at odds."[25]

Price explains that even when feminists and the state seem to be cooperating toward a common goal, each has a different purpose in mind, and she points to the contradiction of gender feminists turning to the state as an ally. "Catharine MacKinnon claims that 'the state is male in the feminist sense.' This means the state views the world from the male perspective. It also means the state uses its ... power to ... protect the interests of men as a gender-class."[26]

Choice is the key to individualist feminism, a tradition that views every woman as a self-owner. Every woman has the inalienable right to use her own body and property in whatever peaceful manner she chooses. Regarding the issue of marriage, individualist feminism reduces it to two key principles: women must retain full control of their own bodies and the state should have no dominion over private sexual arrangements. These two principles are perhaps best illustrated by looking back into history at the lives of the men and women who published the free love periodical *Lucifer, the Light Bearer* (1883–1907) in nineteenth-century America.[27]

The first principle upon which the *Lucifer* circle insisted was that women have full control of their own bodies and, particularly, of their own sexuality. This control was not diminished by marriage. Indeed, *Lucifer* was one of the first voices in America to claim that forced sex within marriage was rape.

On February 23, 1887, a federal marshal arrived in a small Kansas town to arrest the staff of *Lucifer* on 270 counts of obscenity. The charges resulted from the publication of three letters to the editor, all of which advocated women's sexual rights. But the controversy revolved mainly around one letter in particular: the Markland letter, published on June 18, 1886. The author of the Markland letter quoted from correspondence he had received:

> Today's mail brought me a letter from a dear lady friend, from which I quote and query:
> "About a year ago F—- gave birth to a babe, and was severely torn by the use of instruments in incompetent hands ... last night, her husband came down, forced himself into her bed and the stitches were torn from her healing flesh, leaving her in a worse condition than ever. I don't know what to do."

Markland continued by asking a long series of outraged questions:

> Can there be legal rape? Did this man rape his wife? Would it have been rape had he not been married to her? Does the law protect the person of woman in marriage? Does it protect her person out of marriage?... If a man stabs his wife to death with a knife, does not the law hold him for murder? If he murders her with his penis, what does the law do?... Can a czar have more absolute power over a subject than a man has over the genitals of his wife?... Has freedom gender?[28]

For publishing this and the two other letters, Moses Harman was sentenced to five years in a Kansas penitentiary. After serving seventeen weeks, he was released on a technicality, retried without a jury on a slightly different charge, and sentenced to one year. After eight months, he was again released on a technicality. In 1895 Harman was sentenced to one year in prison, which he served in its entirety. Harman's last imprisonment was in 1906; he spent a year at hard labor, often breaking rocks for eight hours a day in the Illinois snow. He was seventy-five at the time.

The second principle upon which the *Lucifer* circle insisted was that the state had no business dictating forms of sexuality or marriage to the individuals involved. Thus, when the marshal arrived to arrest the staff of *Lucifer*, two members were missing—Edwin C. Walker and Lillian Harman, Moses' sixteen year old daughter. The couple had already been imprisoned for their marriage, which had been sanctioned by neither state nor church. The purpose of the marriage had been to declare the right of individuals to form sexual partnerships on their own, without permission from the state or society.

During the marriage ceremony, Lillian had declared: "I enter into this union with Mr. Walker of my own free will and choice.... I ... retain the right to act, always, as my conscience and best judgment shall dictate. I retain, also, my full maiden name, as I am sure it is my duty to do."[29] The ceremony ended with Moses Harman refusing to give away the bride for he wished her always to be the owner of her own person.

News of this marriage without state sanction drew threats of mob violence. When a relative brought a complaint against the couple, city officials arrested Lillian and Edwin. They were charged with unlawfully and feloniously living together as husband and wife without being married according to statute. Edwin was sentenced to seventy-five days in jail, Lillian to forty-five. Before sentencing, the judge asked if there was any reason why the sentence should not be passed. Lillian replied: "Nothing. Except that we have committed no crime. But we are in your power, and you can, of course, do as you please."[30]

Gender feminists would maintain that the state had a right and even an obligation to intervene in the terms of Lillian's sexual/marriage contract.

Indeed, gender feminists, such as Carole Pateman, argue that the sexual/marriage contract is not a private one at all and should not be treated as such. Sexual contracts are not simply political, they are one of the main ways that patriarchy and capitalism sustain themselves. The sexual contract allows men to form an aristocracy of political and social privilege. In her book, *The Sexual Contract*, Pateman contends: "Political right originates in sex-right or conjugal right. Paternal right is only one, and not the original, dimension of patriarchal power. A man's power as a father comes after he has exercised the patriarchal right of a man (a husband) over a woman (wife)."[31]

Conclusion

Gender feminists and individualists view the same institution—marriage—and come to opposite conclusions. Gender feminists insist that the state must thrust justice into an inherently oppressive condition: marriage and family life. Individualists demand that the state withdraw from marriage and allow the adults involved to work out their own definition of justice in the privacy of their homes.

To individualists, the state is already too intimate a partner in everyday life. Modern marriage contracts are not agreements between a husband and wife so much as they are three-sided arrangements between a husband, a wife, and the state. That is, the state legally defines what a marriage is and how it can be dissolved. Without government approval—in the form of a divorce decree from the court—a marriage cannot be terminated.

In essence, the state has a controlling interest. And the state must bear a great deal of the blame for the current evils of marriage.

Individualist feminists agree that a revolution is necessary, but one that gives power to individuals and not to institutions, such as the state. Women need liberation, not state control. In essence, marriage must be taken out of the political realm and returned fully to the private one. The new slogan of feminism should be, "The personal is personal." In marriage, as in all other peaceful pursuits of life, let individuals choose.

Notes

1. Laura Levin, "The Changing Role of the Family," in *Violence in the Home: Interdisciplinary Perspectives*, ed. Mary Lystad (New York: Brunner/Mazel, 1986), pp. 32–33.

2. Florence Rush, "The Many Faces of Backlash," in *Sexual Liberals and the Attack on Feminism*, p. 173.

3. Catharine MacKinnon, "Liberalism and the Death of Feminism," in *Sexual Liberals and the Attack on Feminism*, pp. 3–4.

4. Friedrich Engels, *The Origins of Family, Private Property, and the State* (Moscow: Progress, 1948), p. 49.

5. Connie Brown and Jane Seitz, "You've Come a Long Way Baby," in *Sisterhood Is Powerful: An Anthology of Writings from the Women's Liberation Movement*, ed. Robin Morgan (New York: Random House, 1970), p. 5.

6. Karl Marx, *Capital*, vol. 1 (Middlesex: Penguin, 1976), p. 719.

7. Nicole Cox and Silvia Federici, *Counter-Planning from the Kitchen: Wages for Housework* (Bristol: Falling Wall Press,), pp. 4–5.

8. Sonia Johnson, "Taking Our Eyes Off the Guys," in *Sexual Liberals and the Attack on Feminism*, p. 57.

9. The Writing Collective, "Sex Resistance in Heterosexual Arrangements," in *Sexual Liberals and the Attack on Feminism*, p. 145.

10. Beverly Jones, "The Dynamics of Marriage and Motherhood," in *Sisterhood Is Powerful*, p. 59.

11. Dallas Costa, *The Power of Women and the Subversion in the Community* (Bristol: Falling Wall Press, 1972).

12. Del Martin, *Battered Wives*, rev. ed. (San Francisco: Volcano Press, 1981), p. 41.

13. Gloria Steinem, *Revolution from Within: A Book of Self-Esteem* (Boston: Little, Brown, 1992), pp. 259–261.

14. Linda Gordon, *Heroes of Their Own Lives: The Politics and History of Family Violence* (New York: Viking, 1988), p. 251.

15. As quoted in "An Orgy Over Whether All Men Are Vile," by George Bain, *Maclean's*, December 23, 1991, p. 48.

16. Ibid.

17. Sommers, *Who Stole Feminism?*, pp. 194–195.

18. Lenore E. A. Walker, "Psychology and Violence Against Women," *American Psychologist*, April 1989, p. 695.

19. Lenore Walker, *The Battered Woman* (New York: Harper Collins, 1980), p. xv.

20. Ibid., p. 98.

21. Steve Metzger, "The Shooting of Josh Wagshall," *Transitions* 8 (2) (March/April 1988): 2.

22. Susan Moller Okin, *Justice, Gender, and the Family* (New York: Basic Books, 1989), pp. 124–125.

23. Ibid., p. 127.

24. Ibid., p. 181.

25. Lisa S. Price, *In Women's Interest: Feminist Action and Institutional Change* (Vancouver: Women's Research Center, 1988), p. 46.

26. Ibid.

27. Free love (along with abolitionism) was the nineteenth-century movement that embodied and advanced individualist feminism.

28. *Lucifer, the Light Bearer*, June 18, 1886.

29. As quoted in Hal D. Sears, *The Sex Radicals: Free Love in High Victorian America* (Lawrence, Kansas: Regents Press, 1977), p. 85.

30. Ibid., p. 92.

31. Carole Pateman, *The Sexual Contract* (Stanford: Stanford University Press, 1988), p. 3.

CHAPTER NINE

Prostitution

Prostitution is the inverse of rape. A prostitute not only controls the exchange of sex, she also benefits financially. To gender feminists, however, prostitution is an act of violence against women as a class: it is "sexual colonization." By throwing up the specter of white slavery—which does not exist in the United States—gender feminists justify their call for eliminating the oldest profession. When sex workers protest, they are cavalierly dismissed as being blinded by oppression. Apparently, it is "a prostitute's body, but not a prostitute's right." Yet prostitutes, who are the most stigmatized women within society, are the ones who most need protection and respect.

Historical Perspective

Perhaps the most common statement about prostitution is that it is the oldest profession. But, since the first prostitute presumably had paying clients, there is reason to doubt whether this claim, as so many others about prostitution, has any validity at all. The clients had to earn their money somewhere.

The label oldest profession does convey something accurate, however: prostitution has been an aspect of virtually every human society since the dawn of time. Some percentage of women have always traded sex; some men have always been willing to pay for it. Different societies have viewed prostitution in widely divergent ways. Some cultures stoned prostitutes to death. In ancient Greece, however, prostitutes were an integral part of religious rites. In Napoleonic France, courtesans were educated and talented women. They were not simply respected; they were adored and often eagerly sought out as wives. Other societies have grudgingly tolerated prostitution as a safeguard for the family. It was deemed to prevent rape and to shield virtuous wives from the unsavory sexual appetites of their husbands. In times of war, many governments have encouraged prostitution in order to provide a sexual release for soldiers away from home.

The feminist movement has also expressed different opinions on the issue of prostitution. The pioneering eighteenth-century British feminist Mary Wollstonecraft considered street prostitution to be a more honest pursuit than marriage, which she called "legal prostitution." More than a century later, the American socialist feminist Emma Goldman maintained "it is merely a question of degree whether [a woman] sells herself to one man, in or out of marriage, or to many men."[1]

Still other feminists, who were involved in the purity crusades that characterized the Progressive Era, vilified prostitution. In her essay *Not Repeating History*, the contemporary feminist Gail Pheterson, who is an advocate for prostitute rights, reflects on the advice offered by Josephine Butler. Butler was a nineteenth-century British radical who championed the rights of prostitutes:

> In 1897, Butler warned her political associates to "...beware of purity workers (who are) ... ready to accept and endorse any amount of coercive and degrading treatment of their fellow creatures in the fatuous belief that you can oblige human beings to be moral by force."[2]

What Is Prostitution?

Why does prostitution elicit such varied reactions? What is prostitution? A descriptive definition is relatively easy to provide: prostitution is the exchange of sexual services for money or other material consideration. But this description does not explain the controversy that has clouded prostitution throughout history. It is a controversy that often reveals more about the ideology of a society than it does about prostitution itself. Equally, the debate within feminism over the issue tends to reveal ideological conflicts within the movement itself.

Liberal feminism tends to stand on one side of this debate, the side favoring prostitutes' rights. Still riding the wave of tolerance that swept the '60s and '70s, liberals tend to view prostitution as a victimless crime, that is, as an activity in which all parties are consenting adults and one that is a crime only because it offends the moral sensibilities of uninvolved and uninjured third parties. Some liberals carry tolerance one step farther into advocacy. They defend prostitution as an extension of the right of consenting adults to perform whatever sexual acts they wish.

Individualist feminists, arguing from the principle of self-ownership, also champion the rights of prostitutes. To them, prostitution is the inverse of rape, during which a woman's body is taken without her consent. In prostitution, a woman fully consents to sex and often initiates it. If society respects a woman's right to say no to sex, it must respect her right to say yes.

There is a difference, of course, between prostitution and regular consensual sex. Prostitution is not merely an exchange of sexual favors; it is a financial exchange. At this point, individualist feminists rise up to defend the free market as well as a woman's self-ownership. A popular slogan of theirs is: "Prostitution is a combination of sex and the free market: which one are you against?"

Both liberal and individualist feminists view prostitutes as women in control of their own sexuality, that is, prostitutes set the price, the timing, and the circumstances of the sexual exchange. So what is the problem? Is Camille Paglia correct when she states that "the prostitute is not, as feminists claim, the victim of men, but rather their conqueror?"[3]

Paglia sees the real problem with prostitution arising from the hypocrisy and double standards of society. The current second-class status of prostitutes is a reflection of American puritanism more than of anything inherent in the profession. Our society tells women to marry well, to get things from men, and to use flirtation to gain favors. Advertising presents sex as a commodity, as part of the medium of exchange. Prostitution is just the logical extension of this societal attitude. But because prostitutes flagrantly express attitudes that are usually left unstated, they are reviled.

To a point, gender feminists agree: society is to blame, not the prostitutes. More specifically, male-dominated society—as expressed through capitalism and patriarchy—is to blame. But this realization does not sway them toward advocating the rights of prostitutes, quite the contrary. Gender feminists seek to eliminate the oldest profession because it is a creation of patriarchy and thus an act of violence against women as a class.

In her essay, "Prostitution in Contemporary American Society," JoAnn L. Miller explains how a seemingly voluntary exchange is actually an act of force:

> Prostitution involves one gender's taking advantage of its superior social status and manipulating the other gender.... Because members of this

less powerful group are compelled or forced, physically or psychologically to engage in a sexual act, prostitution is fundamentally coercive and exploitative.[4]

Prostitution, it is claimed, legitimizes the social attitudes that subjugate women as a class. Thus, prostitutes have a moral and political obligation to stop selling their bodies because these transactions fortify the cultural assumptions that damage women. These assumptions are said to have dire consequences. Specifically, prostitution is said to lead to rape. Thus, prostitutes are contributing to the rape culture.

In her pioneering book *Against Our Will*, Susan Brownmiller insists:

> The case against toleration of prostitution [is] central to the fight against rape, and if it angers a large part of the liberal population to be so informed, then I would question in turn the political understanding of such liberals and their true concern for the rights of women.[5]

The Gender Feminist and the Prostitute

Gender feminists view prostitutes either as victims of capitalism who must be saved—against their will if necessary—or as enemies who "open up their legs to patriarchy." Two questions immediately arise: (1) If prostitution is violence against women, why would any woman choose to enter that trade?; and, (2) If a woman does choose to sell her sexual services, how can feminists dismiss her choice to use her own body as she sees fit? Gender feminists respond to the first question in basically two ways. Both responses deny that the prostitute has truly chosen her profession. First, gender feminists claim that women become street prostitutes through a brutal process by which they are kidnapped and forced to perform sexual acts. This is the white slavery that Gail Sheehy's influential book *Hustling* portrays.

White slavery is clearly a serious problem in Third World countries, especially Asian countries, but no convincing evidence points to the existence of a similar problem in the United States. Even if white slavery were flourishing in the U.S., however, it is an activity quite distinct from prostitution, a criminal activity already prohibited by laws against kidnapping. White slavery involves kidnapping women and forcing them to perform sexual acts. Prostitution involves consenting adults performing sexual acts for mutual profit. If white slavery were swept away, prostitution would still continue.

Second, gender feminists further claim that under capitalism, women's choices are limited to wage slavery, domestic slavery, or sexual slavery (prostitution). None of these alternatives could be called choices in any meaningful sense of that word. They are simply rules dictated by a male-dominated culture. As Alison Jaggar explained, "it is the economic coercion underlying prostitution,... that provides the basic feminist objection to prostitution."[6]

Despite such clear statements, the issue of prostitution has a complicated history within the gender feminist movement. In the late seventies, when radical theory was being pounded out, some voices actually eulogized prostitution. Ti Atkinson, for one, considered prostitutes to be paradigms of the sexually liberated woman. By the '80s, however, many feminists had become disillusioned with sexual liberation. Violence against women—on the street and in the home—seemed to be escalating. The wage gap remained the same. Abortion rights were being challenged on the state level in many areas of the country. As some feminists looked back over the '70s and the '80s, they concluded that sexual liberation was a fraud. At this point, gender feminism developed a cohesive stand on the issue of prostitution, declaring prostitutes victims of patriarchy and prostitution, in and of itself, an act of violence.

In recent years, the position on prostitution has evolved yet again. More and more, gender feminists are starting to show sympathy toward prostitutes as victims while becoming more understated about their goal of eliminating prostitution itself. After all, they argue, in a male-dominated world where most women must choose between wage labor and domestic labor, some women will say no to both and choose prostitution instead. Prostitution is now seen as a paradigm of woman's dilemma under patriarchy.

Gender feminist Evelina Giobbe explains how white males in the conservative right and the liberal left "collude" to keep women in prostitution: "The right by demanding that women be socially and sexually subordinate to one man in marriage, and the left by demanding that women be socially and sexually subordinate to all men in prostitution and pornography."[7]

Some gender feminists even seem to accept the possibility of prostitution being a valid pursuit, that is, if certain political conditions are met first. These conditions are economic equality between the sexes; and equal numbers of women and men buying the services. In other words, prostitution *might* be valid after a gender feminist revolution establishes socioeconomic equality; and after the sex trade has adopted affirmative action.

Other gender feminists seem to be playing a game of semantics. For example, in her book *Female Sexual Slavery*, Kathleen Barry begins by defining slavery (specifically sexual slavery) in such broad terms that few professions could escape that label. She claims:

> Female sexual slavery is present in ALL situations where women or girls cannot change the immediate conditions of their existence; where regardless of how they got into those conditions they cannot get out; and when they are subject to sexual violence and exploitation.[8]

Consider Barry's words: "women or girls [who] cannot change the immediate conditions of their existence." This definition of sexual slavery includes anyone who relies on a regular paycheck, regardless of their occupation. After all, what women or girls can "change the immediate conditions of their existence"? The borders of Barry's definition are so vague that virtually any activity she wishes to label could thus be called sexual slavery.

Barry's subsequent call for the "decriminalization" of prostitution appears to be a defense of a woman's right to use her own body, that is, of the right to contract. But is it? At this point, Barry displays the joker in her deck. She makes it clear that the perceptions of prostitutes themselves as to whether they are consenting are unimportant. In other words, however much an adult prostitute of sane mind may proclaim her desire to remain a prostitute, her voice need not be taken seriously. Like a child or a mentally incompetent person, she has no right to control her own body and no claim on its disposition.

If she does not, then who does? Barry explains: "And I assume that we must determine a woman's ability to freely enter or leave institutions of sex colonization based on her actual conditions and not simply on her perception of them or her desire to participate regardless of the conditions."[9] The "we" in Barry's theory is not defined. Presumably, either society, the state, or gender feminists will decide for the prostitute.

Thus, a prostitute who is deemed to be a victim will not be allowed to stay in the profession. This is a Catch-22: a prostitute who wants to stay in the profession is psychologically unhealthy and should be forced to leave it. A prostitute who wants to leave the profession is psychologically healthy and may well be allowed to stay. In holding this position, Barry is playing word games similar to those of other gender feminists who state that prostitutes should not be arrested but that they should be forced to receive rehabilitative therapy so that they will no longer wish to be prostitutes.

What would this rehabilitation look like? Barry's ultimate solution is to have women transcend a male-dominated culture and the "valueless individualism" of liberal intellectuals. Barry contends that liberal individualism has no values attached to it, that is, it tells people to pursue self-fulfillment without telling them what specific paths are acceptable.

Instead, Barry wants to reclaim a world in which more rigid values exist. She wishes to

> reclaim the need for values—not values as they *had* been, but values that stem from new definitions of what is right and wrong, what is enhancing to human beings versus what is demeaning, and what leads to a positive valuation of life versus what tends toward destruction and dehumanization.[10]

It is difficult to imagine how prostitution can survive such a defense. Nevertheless, it is a sign of the times that gender feminism is offering any defense whatsoever.

Sex Workers Against Gender Feminists

Much of the change within gender feminism comes from the fact that, in the last decade, prostitutes and other sex trade workers have organized politically. Organizations like COYOTE—Call Off Your Old Tired Ethics—have spoken out against their critics, including feminists. Such organizations of prostitutes and their advocates have forced gender feminists to come face to face with the women they supposedly want to help. Gender feminists have been forced to realize that these women view them as the enemy.

Historically, prostitutes have good reason to feel such animosity. The International Committee for Prostitutes' Rights explains:

> Historically, women's movements ... have opposed the institution of prostitution while claiming to support prostitute women. However, prostitutes reject support that requires them to leave prostitution; they object to being treated as symbols of oppression and demand recognition as workers.[11]

In short, prostitutes demand respect from feminists, not pity or condescension. But more than this, prostitutes demand to be taken seriously. After all, they are the ones with firsthand experience of the trade. Many of them vigorously dispute the gender feminist caricature of the prostitute as a humiliated and degraded victim of men.

In speaking of the book she coauthored, *We Are Women Like All Women*, prostitute Pieke Biermann claims that feminists do not want to learn from prostitutes. Gender feminists have already neatly analyzed the problem and have reached the answer they desire. Indeed, they have reached the *only* conclusion they are willing to accept, namely, that patriarchal capitalism is to blame. In pursuit of this foregone conclusion, gender feminists draw only on those accounts, studies and statistics that support their position. They credit the experiences of victims such as Linda Lovelace and discount the experiences of self-determining prostitutes such as Norma Jean Almodovar, author of *From Cop to Call Girl.*

Gender feminists publish the statements of organizations such as WHISPER—Women Hurt in Systems of Prostitution Engaged in Revolt—a national organization of women who have survived the sex industry, while ignoring the voice of proprostitute groups like COYOTE. The probability is high that both views of the sex industry have validity. A trade that is driven underground and denied protection by the law almost invites the victimization of those who engage in it. On the other hand, any trade that reaps huge profits and allows substantial worker control attracts strong, competent workers who refuse to be victims. The paradox of prostitution is that both descriptions apply to it equally.

However, to reach the conclusions they desire, gender feminists can credit only one side of the story. Women who are not victims must be considered liars, fools, or mentally incompetent. Understandably, prostitutes who do not feel victimized resent the feminists who so contemptuously ignore them. In addressing feminist Susan Cole from the floor of a conference, one prostitute complained: "I listened to you talk and use the fact that we're violated in our work environment to give some sort of legitimacy to your argument. You've made it very clear that you don't want to talk to politicized whores or politicized porn workers."[12] The prostitute accused gender feminists of dishonesty: "This is the problem that we've been facing continually. You only use the gutter stories to back up your position. Let's stop the victim shit.... Let's recognize that we're not crippled as women in this industry. We are capable of exercising a healthy control over our own environment."[13]

Gender feminists are ideologically committed to *not* listening to prostitutes who defend their profession. And prostitutes are well aware of the short shrift they are receiving. As CORP (Canadian Organization for the Rights of Prostitutes) explains:

> When you have a prostitute that says, "Well, I don't agree with the way you're interpreting my life, I don't feel oppressed or I don't feel exploited in the way that you're saying," [feminists] say things like, "She's too blinded by her own oppression to see her experience."[14]

According to CORP, gender feminists then add insult to injury: "They find it necessary to interpret prostitutes' experience of their lives and then feed it back to the prostitutes to tell them what's really happening, whereas they wouldn't dare be so condescending or patronizing with any other group of women. Why is that?"[15]

The Advantages of Prostitution

A brief discussion of the results of a survey I conducted of prostitutes in COYOTE follows in chapter 10. Prostitutes chose their line of work because it offers real advantages. The most obvious advantage is money. Prostitutes can earn a great deal, especially compared to the income of the average working woman. The prostitute's income is enhanced by the fact that it is "tax-free."

Although money is often the overriding motive behind prostitution, other factors can figure in a woman's decision to sell her sexual services. Jennifer James's acclaimed study (1976) of New York prostitutes listed many motives prompting women to become whores, such as a desire for independence, a sense of adventure, and the lure of the madonna-whore myth.

Prostitution is doubly attractive to poor and underprivileged women because it does not require a great deal of education, skill, or training. Moreover, it is neither boring nor routine, like waitressing or working in a factory. Indeed, some prostitutes speak of meeting interesting people and of the warm bonds they develop with other women in the trade. Others claim to learn about themselves through sexual contact with clients. Perhaps this is because the control the women exercise over the encounter can remove inhibitions, fears, and guilt.

Some studies have concluded that many prostitutes enjoy their work. Other studies have reported that most white female prostitutes chose the profession because they disliked the discipline of conventional work, not because they were forced to or had emotional problems.[16]

In short, prostitution offers a large degree of worker control. Like any other business person, prostitutes set their own prices within the bounds of the marketplace. Unlike most professionals, prostitutes can drop in and out of the business without losing any earning power. They can set the hours they work. This is particularly important for women who have small children or other consuming family demands.

In short, the job is both individualistic and largely under the control of women. This individualism is reflected in the antipathy many prostitutes show toward a commonly offered "solution" to prostitution: state control of the industry. For prostitutes, state-run brothels have major drawbacks: women are not able to set their own hours and fees or to refuse clients. In essence, prostitutes become sexual civil servants and brothels become government sex factories.

Prostitutes want independence. They want to be taken seriously as workers. They want respect from the feminist movement, which means being viewed as the equals they are. Most campaigns for prostitute rights already carry a feminist stamp, and many prostitutes identify with feminist values, such as independence, financial autonomy, sexual self-determination, personal strength, and female bonding. They should be the natural allies of feminists. And they may be the one class of women who most need the feminist movement; prostitutes desperately need a strong political ally to shield them from the real dangers of the profession.

As it is, prostitutes have had to handle most of their own problems with little help from feminism. This is particularly true of street prostitutes who, as the lowest paid and most visible of the profession, are the most stigmatized. These are the women most persecuted by the police. They are left with no protection against violence or disease. These women need feminists to champion their rights. It is, however, left to organizations, like COYOTE, to bring these women out of the political backwaters of society.

The Right to Contract

The most basic question of prostitution is whether a woman has the right to sell her sexual services, to use her body as she sees fit. Prostitutes certainly think so; in fact, they claim the services they sell do not differ in kind from those sold by most working women. Surgeons sell the skill of their hands; writers sell their talent with words; lawyers sell their legal advice—prostitutes sell their sexual services.

Eva Rosta, an English prostitute, makes this point clearly: "We know about economics, we know about the social sides and sexual sides, we know what's going on ... all work involves selling some part of your body. You might sell your brain, you might sell your back, you might sell your fingers for typewriting."[17] Rosta concludes, "I choose to sell my body the way I want to and I choose to sell my vagina."[18]

In other words, prostitution is a matter of contract. It is a barter of sexual favors for material consideration. A prostitute trades her sexual services like a secretary trades her typing services. Both are using their bodies to engage in a commercial transaction. Those who object to prostitution because it reduces women to sexual objects or body parts must logically object to a wide range of other activities that do the same, including modeling, professional athletics, and acting.

Gender feminists take a different approach to prostitution. To the basic question of whether a woman has the right to sell her sexual services, to use her own body as she sees fit, they answer no. Some avoid the question of a woman's right to contract by defining the act of prostitution, in and of itself, as violence. Since there can be no such thing as a contract to steal, rape, or otherwise violate rights, this redefinition obviates any need to deal with the sticky issue of the prostitute's consent.

Other gender feminists simply deny that prostitutes have any right to contract at all, since this so-called right is one of the weapons patriarchy uses to oppress women. There can be no such thing as the right to contribute to women's oppression. Carole Pateman expresses this clearly in her book, *The Sexual Contract*: "Prostitution is an integral part of patriarchal capitalism. Wives are no longer put up for public auction ... but men can buy sexual access to women's bodies in the capitalist market. Patriarchal right is explicitly embodied in 'freedom of contract.'"[19]

Liberal and individualist feminists argue that the right to contract is a direct expression of "a woman's body, a woman's right." How can this principle oppress women? Pateman explains that a woman's self-ownership is precisely what enslaves her. "The subject of all the contracts with which I am concerned is a very special kind of property, the property that individuals are held to own in their persons."[20] She concludes, "the individual as owner is the fulcrum on which modern patriarchy turns."[21]

In other words, the right to contract and the principle "a woman's body, a woman's right" form the fulcrum of the oppression of women by men. If women are to be liberated, both contracts and self-ownership must be denied. Gender feminists have turned away from contract and self-ownership toward regulation and government control.

This attitude stands in direct opposition to granting full rights and responsibilities to women. Nevertheless, it is to the government that gender feminism *must* turn if it wishes to eliminate the choice to become a prostitute. No other mechanism in society has the power to do so.

Differing Solutions to Prostitution

Traditionally, society has approached "the problem" of prostitution in three general ways:

1. Suppression: government has attempted to prohibit all acts of prostitution, as well as the activities that promote it, such as keeping a brothel;

2. Regulation: government has forced prostitutes to register with

the police and subjected them to rules meant to protect health and public decency;

3. Tolerance: all laws against prostitution have been abolished, though laws against associated activities, such as public solicitation, have sometimes been upheld.

Most feminists advocating prostitutes' rights do not favor regulation, which would do little more than institutionalize the worst aspects of the profession. Prostitution would operate aboveboard, but it would be illegal to sell sex except on the government's terms, prices, venues, etc. Thus the control of the individual worker would vanish without necessarily eliminating the associated stigma. If other attempts at decriminalization can be used as a standard, prostitutes' incomes would be taxed; yet prostitutes probably could not claim social benefits or workers' rights since prostitution would not be viewed as a form of employment. Nor could prostitutes claim health benefits. They would be required to submit to frequent medical examinations, but they could not choose their own doctors. Special laws against venereal disease would be enforced against prostitutes and, as a trade, they would be unique in requiring medical certificates. Regulation would isolate, weaken, and silence prostitutes. It is a mystery as to how regulation could either protect or empower women. It merely empowers the state.

The true feminist approach to prostitution is to advocate the abolition of all laws against it. There are several reasons for this:

1. Laws against prostitution have historically been used to harass and oppress women in the sex industry, not the men who are customers. This means that laws against prostitution almost amount to de facto laws against women. Even laws against pimps (assumed to be men) only add to the persecution of prostitutes. This is because pimping is defined in economic terms; a pimp is merely an associate of a prostitute who receives any of her earnings. It has nothing to do with whether or not the woman is forced to perform sex. This definition of a pimp is so broad it includes roommates, lovers, male adult children, and friends. The associates of prostitutes are often rounded up under the charge of pimping. This violates the prostitute's right of free association.

Moreover, since pimps are almost always defined as "those habitually in the company of prostitutes," antipimping laws interfere with the prostitute's right to marry. A husband would automatically open himself up to charges of pimping.

2. Laws against activities associated with prostitution also become de facto laws against women, for example, laws against running a brothel. In 1949 the General Assembly of the United Nations adopted a legal guideline

ostensibly meant to protect prostitutes. The document, entitled "Convention for the Suppression of the Traffic in Persons and of the Exploitation of the Prostitution of Others," read in part:

> The parties to the present convention further agree to punish any person who:
> Keeps or manages, or knowingly finances or takes part in the financing of a brothel;
> Knowingly lets or rents a building or other place or any part thereof for the purpose of the prostitution of others.

Such laws effectively deny prostitutes the right to work indoors in a warm, safe, and clean place. They also make it difficult for women to band together for safety because those who work in tandem could be charged with running a brothel. Antibrothel laws make prostitutes isolated and vulnerable.

3. Antiprostitution laws ensure that prostitutes will be unable to report violence committed against them to the police. Because the complaints come from criminals, they are almost never taken seriously or pursued. Even the murder of a prostitute is rarely investigated properly. On the contrary, prostitutes who complain to the police are likely to be further abused. Margo St. James claims that 20 percent of the violence against prostitutes comes from pimps, 20 percent from police, and 60 percent from clients—about whom prostitutes cannot complain to the police. Prostitutes receive no protection from the state, even though they give a fortune to it in paying off fines.

4. Criminalizing prostitution has driven the profession underground and resulted in horrible working conditions for the women involved. Its black market nature attracts other illegal activities to the trade. This, in turn, creates a vicious cycle. For example, the stigma and awful working conditions of prostitution drive women to drugs, which are then cited as a reason to strengthen laws against prostitution. Yet drug addiction is a problem that can be linked to many professions, not least among them the medical profession. Only in the case of prostitution are laws enacted against the trade as a whole.

5. Antiprostitution laws function as a form of censorship against women, because they keep prostitutes from speaking up for fear of being targeted by police. In Europe, for example, many countries stamp the passports of prostitutes to identify them as such. Other countries may refuse to admit them. This serves to restrict the prostitute's travel and activities. To avoid being branded, prostitutes lie or keep silent. Speaking out might result in losing custody of their children and opening up lovers

and friends to charges of pimping. In some countries, everything a prostitute owns can be taken away from her as the proceeds of illegal activity. Such repression also hinders the ability of prostitutes to organize politically.

6. To the extent that prostitution creates a public nuisance, laws already exist to prevent these problems. The most commonly cited public nuisances include: children may have to walk by prostitutes and so suffer psychological trauma; prostitutes may destroy the image and safety of a neighborhood; they cause noise and fights during the night; nonprostitutes may be more vulnerable to harassment due to the presence of whores.

Feminists should realize that public nuisance arguments for antiprostitute laws are smoke screens. These laws are not aimed at removing a nuisance, namely, what prostitutes do, e.g., cause noise or disturbances. They are aimed at removing what prostitutes *are*—women who sell sex. This is clear from the many antiprostitute ordinances that require no evidence of bad behavior for a charge to be brought. After all, any real nuisance a prostitute creates could be dealt with under existing public order laws that make it illegal to publicly hurl threats, abuse, or obscenities. The purpose of antiprostitution laws is to target a specific category of women for persecution.

As for straight women who are afraid to be out at night, the real problem lies not with the prostitutes but with the men who harass and/or physically abuse *any* woman. Male violence cannot be blamed on prostitutes, any more than domestic violence can be blamed on wives.

If gender feminists are concerned with the safety and dignity of women, they should join hands with prostitutes and help them to walk out of the shadows in which they now live and work. They should cease to feel sorry for prostitutes and start talking to them as equals. Feminists need the insights of prostitutes as much as prostitutes need the political clout of feminists. Prostitutes often face life-threatening problems. And they are being left to deal with them alone. Feminists of all stripes should speak with one voice to demand the safety of these neglected women.

Conclusion

Women's freedom is a seamless web of issues that emanates from one central principle: "a woman's body, a woman's right." Gender feminists seem to acknowledge this principle when they deal with issues such as date rape, where they insist that no means no. If gender feminists wish to oppose rape, by which a woman is taken without consent, they must defend prostitution, by which a woman offers herself with full consent. If no means no, then yes means yes. Gender feminists must take a woman's right to contract seriously. Prostitutes are the natural allies of feminists. Gender feminists must not be allowed to turn them into our enemies.

Notes

1. "The Traffic in Women," in Emma Goldman, *Anarchism and Other Essays* (New York: Dover, 1969), p. 179.

2. Gail Pheterson, ed., *A Vindication of the Rights of Whores* (Seattle: Seal Press, 1989), p. 11.

3. Paglia, *Sex, Art and American Culture*, p. 18.

4. JoAnn L. Miller, "Prostitution in Contemporary American Society," in *Sexual Coercion: A Sourcebook on Its Nature, Causes, and Prevention* ed. Elizabeth Granerholz and Mary A. Koralewski (Lexington, Mass: Lexington, 1991), p. 47.

5. Brownmiller, *Against Our Will*, p. 390.

6. Alison Jaggar, "Prostitution," in *The Philosophy of Sex: Contemporary Readings*, ed. A. Soble (Totowa, N.J.: Rowman and Littlefield, 1980), p. 360.

7. Laurie Bell, ed., *Good Girls, Bad Girls: Sex Trade Workers and Feminists Face to Face* (Toronto: Women's Press, 1987), p. 76.

8. Kathleen Barry, *Female Sexual Slavery* (New York, Avon, 1981), p. 40.

9. Ibid., p. 279.

10. Ibid., p. 266.

11. The International Committee for Prostitutes' Rights (Brussels, October 1–3, 1986), p. 192.

12. As quoted in *Good Girls, Bad Girls*, p. 181.

13. Ibid.

14. Ibid., p. 213.

15. Ibid.

16. "Misconceptions About Female Prostitutes," *Medical Aspects of Human Sexuality* 3 (July, 1969), pp. 28–30. *Women Working: Prostitution Now* by Eileen McLeod (London: Croom Helm, 1982).

17. Pheterson, *A Vindication of the Rights of Whores*, p. 146.

18. Ibid.

19. Pateman, *The Sexual Contract*, p. 189.

20. Ibid., p. 5.

21. Ibid., p. 14.

CHAPTER TEN

Why Do Women Trade Sex for Money?

The following represents some of the results of a survey I conducted of women who are involved in sex work. The women were all members of COYOTE, a national advocacy group for sex workers. COYOTE a (Call Off Your Old Tired Ethics) was originally an advocacy group for prostitutes. Its membership, which is still largely drawn from prostitutes, offers one of the few windows through which one can glimpse the real motivations and experiences of women who are drawn toward sex work. Whether their hunger is for money, exhibitionism, or just sex, the drive within these women is so strong that they risk being jailed and shunned.

In approaching the members of COYOTE, I began with Norma Jean Almodovar, the director of COYOTE. Because we share political concerns, I was deemed trustworthy. She agreed to distribute about two hundred unaddressed, prestamped surveys to chapters who felt comfortable sending them on to members. The following reflects some of the results of that survey.

As a caveat it should be noted that the sex workers surveyed belong to an outspoken political organization: that is my sampling is not random. These are socially aware women, who are successful enough to have time to be political. Moreover, these women are willing to be visible, as evidenced by the surprising number of addresses and phone numbers that were written across the top of the form.

Yet not every member of COYOTE trusted my intentions. A few months later, I found out how much debate my survey had occasioned. One prostitute, a redhead with a striking mane of hair, told me of a call girl who had refused to fill out the survey because she thought it was "a

trick by the police." Even when assured that the anonymous return enve-
lope could not be traced, she stood firm in her suspicions. She was not
going to be duped. And who can blame her? I was asking these women
to trust me when they could conceivably be arrested for doing so. I was
touched by how many women were willing to take a chance on me. All
in all, several dozen surveys were returned, filled with amazing data.

As a second caveat, however, I should clearly state that I conducted
an informal survey, not a controlled study. Such a sampling proves nothing, but it can *dis*prove a great deal. For example, if antisex advocates
assert that all prostitutes are psychologically damaged and I can point to
even one call girl who is not so damaged, their claim is invalidated.

As the mail arrived at my rural address in Canada, I opened the
surveys with more than scholarly interest. I wanted to know about these
women who had chosen a different sexual road.

One of the first questions on my survey was: what is the main attraction
of sex work? One prostitute filled in the blank I provided, then continued her
response on the back of the page, "Couldn't believe I could get paid to have
a good time. Do not misunderstand—it is work—but it lets me have freedom
to live a different lifestyle and do things. And it can be very fun."

One prostitute answered my question as follows:

> I do this because I like it. And, because let's face the hard economic real-
> ity. I can't sit around making 60 cents for every male dollar and hope for
> some cock in shining armor ... 50 percent of marriages end in divorce
> and I will never depend on one man to provide for me.... I can make a
> minimum of $4000 a week and have made $8000 on very good weeks.

Her explanation made sense to me. Men dream of becoming super-
stars who make lots of money and have lots of dates. Women often hunger
and thirst along similar lines: sex they can control with men who will
pay royally to get it from them.

Another sex worker confided: "For an attractive young woman with
only a high school education, the opportunity for financial gain and the
chance to see the world first class on other people's money was extremely
appealing."

A woman new to "the business," who had been sexually abused as a
child, printed neatly, "I have sexual hangups. This allows me to openly hate
some of the men I meet. It's therapeutic." A veteran, who said she had
been "partying hearty" for 25 years, assured me, "Men treat me better when
they pay me. The women I meet can be trusted (a little) better. I can play
dressup and come and go as I please. There's a higher degree of honesty."

In reading through the surveys, I began to discard illusions about women in sex work. Among the conceptions now in my intellectual trash can are:

Myth #1: Sex Workers Are "Dysfunctional Women"

This is the theory that women sex workers are drug addicted, sexually compulsive, neurotic victims of male society. The survey had the following results:

• 95 percent had not been coerced into the industry. The one woman who answered "yes" (she had been coerced) gave a somewhat confusing description of the "coercion." She wrote "a female friend persuaded me. I could kill her now."

• 88 percent had never heard of a woman being coerced into the business. Of the two women who knew of such instances, one referred specifically to street walkers, and the other explained, "I have known many women in this field, but only one that was coerced. When she was twelve years old, her father put her out on the street to supply his drug use."

• 56 percent reported having either "happy" or "average" childhoods. Comments from those with unhappy childhoods sounded remarkably like the complaints of women from every other walk of life: "we moved a lot," "I was painfully shy," "distant from parents."

• 68 percent had not been sexually molested; 76 percent had not been otherwise physically abused.

• 83 percent were more "sexually confident/comfortable" as a result of sex work and made comments such as "I get a lot of good feedback from men." Those women who were "less confident/comfortable sexually" provided reasons such as "I lost the illusion that sex = love," and "I'm less comfortable with a real monogamous relationship."

It became more difficult to view these women as dysfunctional, when so many of them wrote personal messages on the survey as though I were an unsophisticated kid sister they were advising. A madam counseled me:

> It's a trap, Wendy, and I'm a smart woman, so I know this. The money is the primary issue.... But your perception about things changes. I objectify men. They're only a means to an end. I am in control because I'm very adaptive and cunning. I know how to play them, position them to attain my objective. It's like a chess game for me, strategy, move/countermove. It's exciting in that sense because I've been very, very successful. It's about the hustles. That's fun too—a battle of wits, with me the victor.

How could I feel condescending sympathy for women of whom:
- 51 percent had a college education;
- 46 percent were pursuing further education;
- 78 percent had special training, such as dance or art.

The women—some naive, some cynical—on the whole had a balanced perspective of their work, dwelling on the negatives of sex as well as its payoffs. In describing "the disadvantages of sex work," they expanded:

> —The obvious—having sex with men you aren't attracted to can be boring, like any other job.
> —I lead a life in which I do not pursue love relationships with men of a serious nature. I have to keep it secret.
> —Having sex with revolting men.
> —You do become somewhat cynical about the promises that men make and their ability to be faithful in a relationship.

These are common questions that almost every woman asks at some point in her life: How can I trust men? How can I remain independent? Where is sexual happiness? I began to question the illusion that sex workers are fundamentally more sophisticated or remarkably different from most other women.

Myth #2: Sex Workers Have Special Knowledge of Men and Sex

This is the myth that prostitutes have flashing insights about men and sex, insights that are denied to other women. Certainly it is true that they have experiences that are beyond the range of most of us, and, perhaps, they have developed unusual sexual techniques. But sex workers seem to have absorbed the same messages about men and sex as most other women have.

Although 83 percent of my respondents said they were more comfortable with sex as a result of their line of work, most of them expressed skepticism about romance and lasting passion. In response to the question whether their attitudes toward men had changed, 71 percent said yes. The following responses are representative of how they perceive their attitudes have changed:

> —I don't trust them as much. Think they mostly all cheat in relationships.
> —I'm not looking for my knight in a G-string with a great clean cock.
> —I love men, but I understand they are so different from women. Attitudes. How they express themselves. Now I'm a bit of a tomboy (I'm 47). Before I was a girl/girl.

—I still love them (in fact, I'm engaged to be married—for the third time) but they are all little boys.

—I realize that the majority of men are liars, pigs, and good for nothing.

Single women on the dating circuit make the same kind of comments about men. The remarks sex workers made about women struck me as being more unusual. As I read them, I remembered Norma Jean explaining to me that in her years of being on the Los Angeles police force, before becoming a prostitute, she had never had real girlfriends. Only after entering sex work was she able to bond with other women.

Although the question, "Has your sexual orientation changed?" was most often left blank, five women said yes and explained that they had become bisexual. Fifteen talked of how their attitude toward women had changed. They seemed to be appreciative of other women in the business, with comments such as: "I respect and admire them, but they need to be better educated so as to not get emotionally bruised by men and by the Monogamy Myth." "I have a lot more female friends and I don't think of women as competition. Simply because I cannot care less for men."

But, on the subject of "straight" women, sex workers were more defensive. One wrote, "Women who aren't sex workers are judgmental, critical of sex workers." Although 37 percent of the women believed that modern feminism represented them, it was usually for vague reasons such as "women are as valuable as men." The 29 percent who felt unrepresented were far more specific in their reasons, writing in comments such as, "They [feminists] see my job as objectification and exploitation, and I do this by choice." Of the respondents 34 percent expressed confusion about the feminist movement.

In trying to uncover the background of the sex workers—the social factors that had formed these attitudes—I discarded a third illusion.

Sex workers begin as teenagers on the street, who sell their bodies as a way to stay alive. Although 73 percent of the respondents were prostitutes, not a single woman came from the streets. The most common ways these women had entered the business was "through a friend" (29 percent) or by "responding to an ad" (20 percent). As to the age at which the women had entered sex work, the most common answer was at twenty years old. Nevertheless, 10 percent became sex workers in their teens, with the youngest age cited as fourteen years old. Half of the respondents began in their twenties, 32 percent in their thirties; 7 percent entered sex work in their forties, with the oldest age cited being forty-two. Overall, both the mean and the median age for becoming a sex worker was twenty-seven.

Motivations for entering the business varied. On the check list of motivations I offered, the one checked off most often was money (95 percent), with a sense of control coming second (65 percent), and curiosity running a close third (54 percent). When they expanded on their answers in the blank space I provided, the women did not sound bewildered or desperate. They sounded like reasonable people who had made a profitable career move:

>—Why not? I traded sexual favors for financial favors and other conveniences before becoming a pro.
>—A cute guy turned me out. Fucked my brains out and then said, "You know you can have that every night, don't you?" He gave me a list of ten numbers. I called a girlfriend who'd been "out" for a year and she taught me how.
>—I can lay down, have fun, be looked at and have more fun and receive money. I am patient and concerned with a man's needs. A good listener due to being a nurse.

The choice to enter sex work seemed increasingly reasonable as I began to compare the amounts per hour these women had earned prior to entering sex work and what they earned afterward. Even factoring in relatively low-paid sex workers, such as strippers, the figures astounded me. Before entering sex work, the women had earned a mean income of $490 for a forty-one-hour week. If the numbers were crunched differently to reflect the median income, their earnings sank to $385 for a forty-hour week. The types of employment ranged widely from waitress to teacher to archeologist.

After entering sex work, the women earned a mean income of $2,360 for a nineteen-hour week. When calculated for the median, their earnings were reduced to $1,650 for a thirteen-hour week. The types of employment ranged from call girl to masseuse to stripper. In other words, after becoming sex workers, these women made about five times as much money while working less than half the time.

Indeed, the money was so attractive that some women felt trapped by it:

>Now, in my life, sex work for money is not a choice ... responsibilities, credit cards and monthly expenses, which I incurred years ago have still imprisoned me in this business. I would quit tomorrow but risk losing all material gain and want to wait until I am free of personal expenses. The money in the beginning is good, but eventually one starts living above your [sic] means and you are enslaved by a monthly expense account that screams to be paid.

A common complaint among the prostitutes was that they did not have enough work. A woman wrote, "I wish I had more clients and I wish they would call more often from above-average hotels." These were not drug-driven street women living on the edge of survival. They were competent adults who had made an economic choice. Like you or me, they saw an opportunity to live a better life, and they grabbed it. Unlike you or me, they were willing to pay the price of that lifestyle.

Here is where sex workers most clearly differed from other women: they accepted and paid a high price for their "aberrant" lifestyle. When asked about the disadvantages of sex work, the women gave an assortment of answers, including no pension plan, dishonest people, sexually transmitted diseases, having sex with revolting men, fear of being abused by clients, soreness, too many antibiotics, tax evasion, and becoming cynical. But the two disadvantages most commonly cited were "social stigma" (49 percent) and "police" (41 percent).

The women in my survey were painfully conscious of being looked down upon as pathetic or degraded. Their answers to the question, "What is the single greatest misconception people have about sex work? overflowed the blank space provided:

> —That it is degrading and shameful and that the women ... are all air-heads and drug addicts. And that we become hard and jaded because of our work. I think people automatically either feel "sorry" for the misfor-tunate [*sic*] girl who sells her body, or look down on you.
> —I guess it's the streetwalker stereotype—pimp in the background, drugs, sleazy hotel rooms, etc. I've been part of none of the above.
> —That all women in this industry were abused children, or psychologi-cally unable to cope or do something else. That it's not a business an intelligent woman would pursue. I would also like to add that I am an attractive woman, but not drop-dead gorgeous. I have a fair amount of intelligence, a large amount of common sense and have never involved myself with drugs or a pimp.
> —Once a woman has been a sex worker, she is no longer worthy of mar-riage and a normal life. No matter when you quit, they will always think of you as a whore.
> —In my opinion, it is that we have no other ability or skill than lying on our backs.

Perhaps the consensus was best captured by a woman who answered with three words, "that we're trash."

I had designed a series of questions aimed at discovering whether society's attitudes toward sex workers kept them from participating in char-ities or other organizations. If so, this would continue a cycle of isolation.

It should be remembered that the women surveyed were willing to be visible and had displayed an interest in politics by joining COYOTE. Probably no other sampling of sex workers is as likely to reflect an involvement in mainstream activities. Nevertheless, a majority of respondents (73 percent) said they did not engage in political activities other than COYOTE; 46 percent were not involved in charitable causes; 63 percent never attended church. "'HE' lost me long ago," one woman scrawled in the margin. Those who claimed sex work kept them from getting involved (31 percent) gave reasons that ran the gamut from "double life" to "I keep activities separate" to "police record."

The second most commonly cited disadvantage of sex work was "police." This disadvantage cuts deep and in two ways. Sex workers are not only vulnerable to arrest and harassment by police, they are also at the mercy of clients against whom they have no legal recourse. A prostitute who calls the police because she has been beaten or raped or robbed is more likely to be arrested herself than to receive justice. How vulnerable does this make the women? Norma Jean Almodovar spoke to me of her own career as a call girl.

> I have never been a victim of violence since I have been a sex worker. I do not consider myself unusual. If you are on the street and you are dealing with someone who can remain anonymous, it is more likely that people you will encounter will be violent. Women off the street are better able to get information about their client and verify who he really is. This puts him in a position of being identified and he is less likely to be violent. On the street, there is a tremendous amount of violence toward the women.

The lack of anonymity on the part of clients served as a powerful filter against abuse. When asked if, as a sex worker, they had been victims of violence, 71 percent of the women responded no. The 29 percent who checked yes, generally also indicated the violence was perpetrated by a client. One woman talked about police abuse and called the "circumstances too painful to describe in writing." Another prostitute described the consequences of going to the police for protection against an attack:

> I was trying to call a taxi to leave when he hit me. The foreswing broke my nose, the backswing cut my lip with his diamond ring.... This happened at the Beverly Wilshire Hotel in a large suite. I was bleeding profusely. He called security and two men carried me out and threw me on the sidewalk in front. I crossed the street to call the police and two men in plainclothes asked me what I was doing. They showed me their badges and said "Let's go over and talk about it." They questioned the men and the other two girls and surprise—only us girls got arrested!

Another call girl recounted her mistake in asking for help against a client who had pulled a gun:

> The police asked my name and I was afraid the client would access it and my address from the police report. I begged the officer not to ask me because I was afraid of retaliation. He would not accept this, so I gave a fake name. When he discovered it would not verify, he arrested me and I became hysterical. He went on to charge me with disorderly conduct.

Given the police attitude toward prostitution, I was amazed to read that some of the women had policemen as friends, even as clients. When I discussed this strange finding with Norma Jean, she explained that, while vice cops are supposed to make arrests, a lot of them "know that the women are not coerced into this business, they are not causing trouble … so they see an opportunity to use the woman's services—for free sometimes, sometimes more honestly."

Confronted by the clear disadvantages of sex work, a key question remained to be answered: do you want to quit? To this 44 percent replied "no"; 24 percent were not sure; 17 percent wanted out. One of the women in the last category wrote, "but not at the price of waitressing." How long did the women expect to remain in sex work? Of the respondents 24 percent of the women said "as long as possible." Most of the others simply did not know.

When asked about their dreams, about what their ideal job would look like, several women replied, "This is it." Most of the responses, however, ran the gamut of possibilities. Some dreams were whimsical and exotic, as with the call girl who declared: "I'd like to be a writer/actress with an agent/manager who'd call me in northern Italy or Micronesia or wherever to show up for a great gig or TV promotion now and then." Other women had more modest, practical dreams, including: owner of a coffee house/dessert café, mother and homemaker, public relations, a darling for a rich intelligent man, and being an attorney in her own law firm.

But throughout the answers to this question, and to the others for that matter, there was a spirit that was captured by one prostitute's response: "I don't believe much in ideals. I'm going back to school and hope to eventually go into research." After reading through the stack of surveys, I came away with the impression that these sex workers were just women trying to better themselves in a world that offered few ideals. In this, they are difficult to distinguish from virtually every other woman I have met.

CHAPTER ELEVEN

Abortion and Reproductive Technology

Since the second wave of feminism—the current revival, which began in the 1960s—the feminist movement has focused much of its energy on the right of a woman to control her own reproductive functions. In the past, this issue has revolved around the principle of self-ownership: namely, "it is a woman's body, it is a woman's right." And if there is a success story for second wave feminism it is (or was) the prochoice campaign to secure safe and legal abortions for women.

Feminists Against Abortion

The current feminist movement no longer offers an overwhelmingly friendly home for abortion or for any other aspect of reproductive technology. Indeed, the abortion issue has been badly muddied by high-profile gender feminists such as Gena Corea who attack virtually every form of reproductive technology from modern abortion to in vitro fertilization (IVF). Corea accuses abortion and contraception of "removing the process of reproduction itself from women."[1] Corea, in attacking reproductive technologies, insists that "we cannot let the ideology that motherhood is a natural need or right stand unchallenged."[2]

But if the right to say yes to motherhood is not a natural one, how can feminists claim a natural right to say no through abortion and birth control? Just as freedom of speech necessarily implies the freedom to remain silent, so too does the right to bear a child involve the right to eschew motherhood. This is a right upon which access to abortion rests.

Corea is not a voice alone. Her views on reproductive technology are becoming more widespread. In her essay "In His Image: Science and Technology," Heather Menzies explains how even birth control—that apparent bastion of women's liberation—is actually part and parcel of women's oppression: "I didn't immediately see the pill or the IUD as sinister in themselves; I began to see them though, in context ... they are part of a particular phrasing of the role of reproduction in society geared to production and consumption, and ... of women's bondage to their own bodies."[3] How has second-wave feminism drifted so far from its roots in the '60s?

Part of the answer is that these roots were liberal, and that ideology no longer dominates the movement. Since the late 1970s, gender feminism has profoundly influenced the ideological direction of the entire movement. Gender feminism is the ideology that regards women's oppression as springing from the twin evils of patriarchy and capitalism. All issues concerning women are processed and analyzed according to this theory.

Although gender feminists are numerically in the minority, their voices are loud and influential. They have managed to virtually define such issues as comparable worth and rape. Regarding abortion, they have either been strangely muted or strangely critical. Some gender feminists state that they are prochoice and then quickly move on to intricate discussions of other matters, such as pornography. Other gender feminists appear to openly attack the prochoice elements within feminism.

In her essay, "Liberalism and the Death of Feminism," Catharine MacKinnon seems unconvinced that legal access to abortion was really a victory for women. For one thing, abortion had been legalized as a privacy right, and gender feminists are inherently suspicious of the private realm in which such perceived outrages as the free market and traditional marriage occur. For gender feminists who rally under the banner "the personal is political," any appeal to privacy rights is merely a mask for patriarchy. MacKinnon writes: "While the women's movement had ... identified the private as a primary sphere of the subordination of women, *Roe v. Wade* had decriminalized access to abortion as a privacy right."[4] Caught up in the enthusiasm of the moment, feminists, according to MacKinnon, forgot themselves: "A movement that knew that the private was a cover for our public condition was suddenly being told—and saying—that the abortion right was our right to the same privacy. If you forgot what this movement knew, this seemed like a good thing."[5]

To the hundreds of thousands of women who claim that the personal is *personal*, that is, to those women who claim that the *Roe v. Wade* decision benefited them as individuals, gender feminists throw a nod of acknowledgment. "Yes," they say, "you did receive an incidental benefit. But, in doing so, you asserted *not* your autonomy, but your place under patriarchy."

Twiss Butler in her essay "Abortion and Pornography" admits that "for any woman who has been able to get the abortion she needed, the benefits of the reform are obvious and genuine."[6] Yet the truth of the issue is quite a different matter:

> Not at all ironically, however, but quite as intended by the men who devised it, granting women a sex-neutral right to privacy in reproductive matters was like granting women expensive, limited, and easily revokable guest privileges at the exclusive men's club called the Constitution.[7]

The pioneering Andrea Dworkin goes one step farther and almost accuses '60s feminists of selling-out. She claims that the right to abortion was merely a bribe contemptuously offered by patriarchy under the guise of liberalism. Dworkin claims that the Left is saying:

> Little girls ... we will allow you to have an abortion right as long as you remain sexually accessible to us. And if you withdraw that accessibility and start talking this crap about an autonomous women's movement, we will collapse any support that we have ever given you.[8]

Dworkin concludes, "And that's what they've been doing to us for the last fifteen years."[9]

The Ideological Reasons for Rejecting Abortion

For months, I have wondered about gender feminism's tendency to criticize rather than to support the prochoice movement. I have concluded that there are basic ideological reasons for the short shrift gender feminism is giving to this issue. These reasons include:

1. The case for prochoice rests on the individualistic principle of self-ownership: "a woman's body, a woman's right." And this principle is antagonistic to the collectivist agenda pursued by gender feminists who emphasize *class* rights and *class* interests. Self-ownership is the foundation of individualism; it is the death knell of class analysis. This is because self-ownership reduces all social struggle to the level of individual rights, where every woman claims autonomy and choice, not as the member of an oppressed subclass, but as a full and free member of the human race.

Such rampant individualism runs against the collectivist grain of gender feminism. To feminists such as Corea, the notion of reproductive choice as a private matter merely contributes to the split between private and public life, which reinforces women's oppression. According to their argument, since women live within a social context, they have an obligation to make decisions that will further women as a class. The individual is less important than the many. In essence, gender feminists wish to alter abortion advocates' most famous slogan to read: "A woman's body, sometimes a woman's right."

2. Prochoice is a call for reform, which is a liberal goal. It is not a call for revolution, which is the radical goal.

In the '60s the campaign for abortion rights was expressed in terms of repeal or legalization. Prochoice advocates wanted to work within the system in order to modify existing institutions. By contrast, gender feminists call for nothing short of a total replacement of the current economic, political, and social system. Prochoice feminists do not say that patriarchal capitalism must be overthrown for women to control their own reproductive functions. They simply state that whatever political system exists, women must have the right to abort a fetus if they so choose. It is difficult to fit this reformist attitude into a revolutionary agenda.

The rhetoric of those opposed to reproductive choice, however, has been so effective that even formerly liberal feminists, who marched for abortion rights and won them, now question whether anything real was achieved. Barbara Katz Rothman epitomizes this drift from the liberal feminism of prochoice to the gender feminism of anti-reproductive technology. She reflects on her transition:

> This emphasis on choice and information all sounded very logical at the time, sounded like women were going to get more and more control as first their access to information and then their choices expanded. I'm beginning to have second thoughts.[10]

3. The success of liberal feminism in securing abortion rights seems to contradict the gender feminist claim that the oppression of women can be corrected only by sweeping away patriarchy. If liberal feminists did score an impressive victory for women without changing the current system, what would happen to this radical claim? In order to maintain their revolutionary vision, gender feminists must deny that the liberals have made meaningful gains.

The core of gender feminism is its opposition to patriarchal capitalism. Every issue in feminism must conform to this political agenda.

Gender feminists deal with abortion as they do with every other feminist issue. Abortion is placed in the much wider context of reproductive technology, which is then placed in the still wider context of patriarchal capitalism. The argument is that for centuries, white male culture has dominated the field of reproduction, which is now being used as yet another way to control women.

To gender feminists, access to abortion is, at best, a token thrown to women to lull them in the false belief they are liberated. At worst, it is medical experimentation and social control conducted by men on the bodies of women. Even reproductive technologies, which were formerly considered to be freedoms, are now called tools of oppression.

In a sense, this approach is inevitable. Gender feminism is an ideology of power and oppression. Power is in the hands of patriarchal males; oppression is the traditional lot of women. This oppression is reflected in every institution of society. Thus, any analysis of reproductive technology by gender feminists will concentrate on the abuse of power by patriarchy.

The Real Abuses of Reproductive Technology

Unfortunately, the gender feminist critique is given credibility by the very real abuses that exist in the area of reproduction. In her essay, "The Future of Motherhood," Elayne Rapping rightfully points out some of the appalling misuses of technology:

> Birth control ... has always been compromised by the social and economic context in which it was developed and distributed. Health risks, unequal access by poor and Third World women, and sterilization abuse of women who want to have more children than society wants them to have are well-known facts.[11]

Gender feminism claims that it is not just poor or Third World women who are disempowered by current birth control; rather, *all* women are oppressed by patriarchal birth control, because it contributes to the political structure by which men subjugate women. Unfortunately, some medical voices seem to support this claim. For example, some doctors advocate performing a cesarean section even against the pregnant woman's will if the fetus's well-being is deemed to require it. In several cases, women who have refused cesarean sections have been compelled to submit to the surgery—under court order and with police escorting them into the operating room.

John Robertson, professor of law at the University of Texas, insists that women who carry children to term acquire certain legal obligations: "These obligations may require her to avoid work, recreation, and medical care choices that are hazardous to the fetus. They also obligate her to preserve her health for the fetus' sake or even allow established therapies to be performed on an affected fetus."[12] Women might be required to do more than avoid risks, however. They might be required to submit to intrusive medical procedures: "Finally, they require that she undergo prenatal screening where there is reason to believe that this screening may identify congenital defects correctable with available therapies."[13]

At the Third National Symposium on Genetics and the Law in Boston in April 1984, Dr. Margery Shaw suggested that child abuse laws be expanded to include fetal abuse.[14] In an earlier essay, Shaw had sketched various scenarios that might constitute fetal abuse, among them the decision to carry a genetically defective fetus to term, the use of alcohol or drugs during pregnancy, improper nutrition during pregnancy, the withholding of prenatal medical care, and exposure to a mother's defective intrauterine environment "caused by her genotype." Thus, according to Shaw, a woman might well have no right to bring a defective fetus to term or even to become pregnant if she is the "wrong" genotype. Moreover, women's eggs may have to meet quality control standards to ensure they are not defective. A woman older than, say, thirty-five, might constitute a "defective intrauterine environment," which jeopardizes the fetus's right to be born sound.

Indeed, a September 1986 report issued by the American Fertility Society—a society of some 10,000 U.S. physicians and scientists—argued that not everyone has the right to reproduce. Among those who may not possess this right are women in overpopulated nations, women unable to care for their children, women with defective genes, and women who might violate proper prenatal care.

Feminists of all stripes are understandably horrified by the possibility of such state control of their reproductive functions. But the gender feminist critique of the new technologies is not based on the fact that they can be abused; rather, gender feminists contend that the technologies are, in and of themselves, abuses committed on the bodies of women. They are inherently oppressive because they have been created and administered by white male culture.

Are Reproductive Technologies Inherently Oppressive?

Today we seem to be on the verge of controlling almost every aspect of the birth process, from conception to genetic determination. New reproductive technologies are removing the constraints nature has placed on reproduction. In the '60s feminists gleefully looked forward to the day when conception could take place without a man. Now that this day has finally arrived, gender feminists maintain that these alleged advances merely give patriarchy enhanced opportunities to control the bodies of women.

A partial list of these supposedly dangerous forms of reproductive technology includes sperm donation, by which a woman conceives with sperm donated from someone other than her spouse or significant other; egg donation, by which a woman conceives with an egg donated by another woman; embryo adoption, by which a donated egg and sperm are cultured into an embryo; embryo freezing; sperm and egg freezing; and embryo screening.

Although infertile women and couples flock to clinics that offer such technology, gender feminists have reacted to these procedures with unalloyed hostility. Consider these statements made by Gena Corea in her essay "The New Reproductive Technologies": "The new reproductive technologies represent an escalation of violence against women, a violence camouflaged behind medical terms…. "Embryo flushing is another of the new reproductive technologies. You artificially inseminate the woman, flush the embryo out of her, and then insert the embryo into another woman. That's done in cows." Concerning surrogacy, she comments, "A man's desire to have a genetically related child becomes a 'medical indication' for buying a woman's body. Such terms sanitize the sale of women and remove the reader emotionally from what is actually going on."[15]

The chorus of criticism is growing. Indeed, reproductive technology has not only been placed in an ideological context, it has also been given a history. In her essay "Feminism, Medicine, and the Meaning of Childbirth," Paula A. Treichler describes the genesis of what she calls "medicalized childbirth": "Certainly productivity in childbearing was linked to the labor-intensive needs of both colonialism and capitalism…. Thus is ideology linked, in turn, to capitalism, industry, and the free market—which provided economic support for medicalized childbirth."[16]

This negative view of technology constitutes something of a shift within gender feminism itself. In 1970 gender feminist Shulamith Firestone, in her pivotal book *The Dialectic of Sex*, suggested that the new technologies would free women: was she wrong? Her contemporary followers think so. They explain that the new reproductive technologies inherently oppress women in two fundamental ways: First and foremost, reproductive technologies have been created by men, who function in the context of patriarchy. This makes the technologies inescapably oppressive to women. The fact that some women and some well-intentioned men may work in this field does not prevent it from being oppressive for the simple reason that individuals cannot change patriarchy by participating in it. Rebecca Albury writes of the new technologies: "Some women have been socialized by the profession. 'Male control' doesn't essentially mean control by individual men, it means control which benefits men more than women most of the time."[17]

Reproductive technology may put on a benevolent face—it may include well-intentioned people—but women should never forget that its goal is subjugation. Gena Corea explains: "We think of medicine as a healing art. But it is not just that. It is also a means of social control or political rule. The word for political rule by physicians is 'pharmacracy.'"[18] Corea dismisses the claim that the new technologies are bringing hope to women who feel devastated by infertility. That, she maintains, is not what these techniques are all about. Such claims are merely "the sugar coating on the pill." Reproductive technologies are about "controlling women, controlling child production, controlling human evolution." Equally important, they are about "making money" and "setting up corporations."[19] Gender feminism's wholesale condemnation of the new technologies extends even to electronic fetal monitors, which have been heralded elsewhere as a breakthrough in fetal care.

The second way in which the new technology is said to oppress women is by marginalizing their role in the birth process. The antitechnologist Janice G. Raymond explains: "As women's reproductive processes become disembodied by the NRTs, this adds another layer to the cultural image that women's bodies are there for the taking—this time by medical technology. The female body becomes ... bound by its use value."[20]

This explanation is typical in its use of Marxist jargon and concepts. Women are said to be "alienated" or "disembodied" from the reproductive faculties of their own bodies. Their bodies are prized for their "use value."

Thus, the "medicalization" of childbirth exploits the body parts of women while making pregnant women almost irrelevant to the process. Gender feminists warn that women are losing the monopoly of power they once enjoyed over the process of giving life. And the final insult is that women are told that the new reproductive techniques give them more—not less—control.

Dismissing Women Who Make the Wrong Choices

When confronted by infertile women to whom reproductive technologies bring hope, gender feminists claim that the opposite is true.

The procedures actually rob them of hope and joy. When women undergo IVF, sex and conception become "a combination of dutiful exercise and competitive sport" in which "sensuality, spontaneity, love" and other technically irrelevant aspects are lost. Whatever benefits individual women believe they have received, the fact is that reproductive technology has damaged these women, both as individuals and as members of a class.

In her essay, "From the Pill to Test-Tube Babies," Elisabeth Beck-Gernsheim explains that the new technologies cannot expand choice because: "Technology is embedded in social institutions, and individual choices are made within a social system that rewards some choices and punishes others."[21] Beck-Gernsheim argues further that the new reproductive technologies violate the democratic process, which is necessary to a free society. In essence, the growth of technology has been so rapid and uncontrolled that it has imposed a new social order on women without having to go through duly elected officials or the process of being put to a vote. Thus, technology is becoming—in and of itself—a form of social control exercised over women.

In analyzing Beck-Gernsheim's argument, it is necessary to assume she truly believes that reproductive technologies, such as abortion, birth control, and IVF, are legitimized by the will of the majority and not by the right of individual women to self-ownership. It is necessary to assume she actually believes that a woman's technological choices concerning her body should be a matter for "duly elected officials."

It is difficult to understand how taking choice out of the hands of individuals and putting it into the palms of politicians can prevent social control. Indeed, the only bastion women have ever had against social control is the self-ownership claim they have in their own bodies, a claim that rightfully withstands the will of the majority, of politicians, or even gender feminists.

Nevertheless, it is precisely self-ownership and individual choice that Beck-Gernsheim attacks:

> The advocates of the new reproductive technologies see their use or nonuse as a matter of individual choice, relating to a person's preferences and responsibility, and emphasize their liberating potential. The critics, in contrast, stress the personal costs and the many new social pressures involved in all forms of modernization.[22]

In the prologue to their book, *Made to Order: The Myth of Reproductive and Genetic Progress*, Patricia Spallone and Deborah Lynn Steinberg make it clear that granting the individual rights to women will damage the class rights of womankind:

> The concept of choice cannot operate outside of the social structures in which it is embedded. The concept of individual rights comes from liberal political theory ... choice is seen as a private matter. This belief contributes to the split between private and public life which reinforces women's oppression.[23]

Again it is claimed, that women cannot truly choose because of the cultural context. It is true that women who decide to use, for example, sperm donation or IVF, have been influenced by their culture. The mere fact that they live in a culture advanced enough to have such procedures influences their choices. As does the fact that in our society women can own property and thus afford such costly technology.

But gender feminists are saying much more than that women are influenced. After all, such a statement would be a truism; it would say no more than that people are affected by their environment, a point no one would argue. Rather, gender feminists are making a two-pronged attack on the possibility of individual modern women making true reproductive choices at all. They are claiming that (1) society has narrowed women's alternatives down to unacceptable choices and (2) given the climate of social oppression, women cannot be held responsible for the apparent choices they make.

Those feminists who refuse to discount the apparent "wrong" choices of women are dismissed and, often, ridiculed. Many gender feminists *do* portray women as incapable of making responsible decisions; at least, women who make "wrong" decisions are portrayed in that manner. Gender feminists, such as Gena Corea, are able to dismiss the choices of "erring" women by insisting that socioeconomic pressures have short-circuited their ability to decide. Indeed, these pressures are so compelling that patriarchy requires no direct use of force to bend women to its will.

In a dystopian view of the future, Gena Corea speculates on the horrors of reproductive technologies and how they will inevitably give over control of women's bodies to men: "They [the new reproductive technologies] will be used to control which kinds of human beings are produced by determining which sperm comes into contact with which egg, which embryos are discarded, which doubled, which altered. When I say this, am I being paranoid?"[24]

Women must not be deceived by men who seem to treat them well or procedures that seem noninvasive. For the face of patriarchy lurks beneath the surface. Corea continues:

> The technologies will be used by physicians for seemingly benevolent purposes. These kindly looking physicians may even speak with a feminist

or a liberal rhetoric, passionately defending a woman's right to choose these technologies and "control her own body."[25]

Corea warns: "It is these good doctors working to reduce human suffering, to create a 'healthier' populace, one more in line with the 'free choices' of women, who are the danger."[26] Apparently, women are so weak-minded that they easily lose the ability to make choices about their own bodies. Fortunately, gender feminists are there to take up the slack.

For gender feminists the bottom line is that birth is a natural process that should take place without medical intervention. Such intervention occurs not to benefit the woman, but to benefit the medical and political establishment. Somehow gender feminist scholarship never incorporates the same statistics that are found in other historical studies. Other studies, for example, of seventeenth- and eighteenth-century Europe when technology and medical intervention in childbirth were rare, show that children had only a 50 percent chance of living until they were twelve months old. Women had a 10 percent chance of dying in childbirth. They had a 20 percent chance of being permanently injured by midwives, who commonly performed such procedures as puncturing the sac of amniotic fluid with their fingernails. Surely all fair attacks on technology and medicine must be balanced against such historical accounts.

Yet gender feminists raise some valid questions that should not be dismissed: Will women have the option to refuse the use of technology? Of special concern is the medical profession's tendency to put the health of the fetus above the autonomy of the pregnant woman. That is, the tendency to force women to undergo unwanted procedures in order to benefit the fetus. Again, this issue hinges on the key question of a woman's right to choose.

An Institution of Reproduction: Technology

In dealing with the sticky issue of choice, it is useful to examine the institution most criticized for coopting women's reproductive freedom, namely, technology or the medical establishment. It is undeniably true that reproductive technologies offer ethical problems as well as practical opportunities. It is also true that the medical establishment—with government support—has a long history of oppressing women.

The persecution of female healers stretches back to the age of witchcraft in Europe. More recently, in the nineteenth century, American doctors persecuted midwives and folk healers while at the same time barring women from universities and other institutions that would have enabled them to enter the more "respectable" ranks of medical practice. Even if the last few decades have seen great strides, no one can blame women for retaining a healthy distrust of the medical establishment. Nor is it difficult to understand their antipathy to the rising rate of hysterectomies, cesarean sections, breast implants, etc., which may well demonstrate a disregard for the well-being of women.

Nevertheless, it must be emphasized again that the gender feminist attack is not based on the actual or possible abuses of the reproductive technologies. Techniques, such as IVF, are not accepted or rejected based on empirical evidence of whether on balance they benefit women. They are rejected because they spring from a particular socioeconomic system. The gender feminist critique of reproductive technology is based on fundamentals. In their essay, "Technology in Childbirth: Effects on Postpartum Moods," Lynne C. Garner and Richard C. Tessler state this clearly: "Advocating economic equity and autonomy, and arguing for appropriate technology distinguish feminist critics of the medical care system from other critics who have focused on the abuses with risky technologies or the excesses of the for-profit orientation."[27]

Gender feminists maintain that the system cannot be reformed because the system, in and of itself, is abusive. Those who believe that science and medicine can be value-free are, at best, naive, for all current knowledge is based on the perpetuation of patriarchal values and assumptions. Therefore, gender feminism aims at nothing less than an intellectual revolution. It seeks to sweep away the new reproductive technologies and, thus, pull one more prop out from under patriarchy. The influential philosopher Sandra Hardin sums up the gender feminist view that science and reproductive technology cannot possibly be value-free:

> It is a system of male-dominance ... where "reproduction" is broadly construed to include sexuality, family life, and kinship formations as well as the birthing which biologically reproduces the species. [The sex/gender system] appears to be a fundamental ... throughout most recorded history and in every culture today.[28]

The Depth of Bias

Technology is only the tip of the oppression. Women are exploited not merely by reproductive technology, but by *all* technology, science, and medicine. Even those developments formerly considered to be advancements for women are now revealed to be oppressive. In his book, *Blaming*

Technology: The Irrational Search for Scapegoats, Samuel C. Florman echoes what has become a gender feminist refrain:

> The development of household appliances ... has helped to reduce her to the level of a maidservant.... Factory jobs have attracted women to the workplace in roles they have come to dislike. Innovations ... such as the baby bottle and birth-control devices, have been developed almost exclusively by men.[29]

Florman concludes that "Dependent upon technology, but removed from its sources and, paradoxically, enslaved by it, women may well have developed deep-seated resentments that persist even in those who consider themselves liberal."[30]

But the roots of the conflict go much deeper than resentment. The debate is ideological and rests on the answers to several key questions, including the following:

1. What is the impact of industrialization and modernization on women?

2. Has technology disrupted what is "natural"?

3. Should services, such as reproductive aid and health care, be broad social responsibilities or commodities on the marketplace?

Advocates of technology maintain that

1. Industrialization has freed women from economic dependence upon their husbands and fathers by offering them a wide range of jobs and educational opportunities. It has also automated and mechanized most household chores, which, admittedly, still seem to fall to women;

2. Technology has disrupted the natural. It has, for example, more than doubled the human life span and greatly decreased both disease and infant mortality. Such disruption has been overwhelmingly positive and should be applauded.

3. Good reproductive aid and health care, like good quality food, can best be provided by a free and competitive marketplace. Moreover, to socialize these services would be, in essence, to socialize the labor of those who provide medical services. It would create a class of public service slaves.

Gender feminists answer that

1. Industrialization has dehumanized women by converting them into low-paid and interchangeable units in the marketplace. It has made them into wage slaves, without removing the domestic burdens they face at the end of each work day;

2. Technology is directly opposed to what is natural, especially in the area of childbirth where medical or scientific intervention is rarely

necessary or desirable. Technology is the direct expression of male thinking, which seeks to dominate and control nature rather than to accept and nurture it;

3. Reproductive aid and health care are too important to become a matter for profit. Such matters are not "services" provided by the marketplace, but basic human rights that should be ensured by the government.

Toward a New Feminist Methodology

For gender feminists the villain behind reproductive technology is modern science. In book after book, patriarchal research and science are critically characterized as controlling the environment rather than being "open" to it, linking validity to reproducible results, relying on evidence rather than on experience, using deductive rather than inductive logic, and seeking to dominate rather than accept. By contrast, feminist research and science is characterized as holistic in its approach to health, woman-centered and opposed to male domination, and offering validation to women's experience.

In her essay, "Theorizing About Theorizing," scholar Dale Spender expands on the extent to which the subjectivity within feminist scholarship is to be embraced: "If everything I know is 'wrong,' that is, if there are no absolutes, no truths, only transitory meanings imposed by human beings in the attempt to make sense of the world, then 'wrong' becomes a meaningless category."[31] Feminist methodology leads Spender to reject the idea of truth as well: "Instead of being frightened that something I am arguing for as truth ... may in fact be wrong, I am starting from the other end and arguing that I know it is temporary and inadequate. I am then searching for the 'errors,' the 'flaws' that will help me to refine."[32]

Spender is saying more than merely that human knowledge is necessarily selective and, thus, subjectivity is inevitable. She is not commenting on the fact that in order to process an almost infinite amount of data, the human brain selects out what it considers important. Such a process is not a matter of intellectual dishonesty. It is part of the inherent functioning of the human mind.

Subjectivity is not bias. It is an inevitable aspect of being human. The accusation of being biased is properly hurled at people who twist evidence in order to arrive at a conclusion they favor. The question is not whether human reason functions selectively but whether the criteria of selection are appropriate. The real questions are whether the selected facts are true and the method of selection is valid. Bias comes into play only when human beings refuse to approach evidence with honesty and to reconsider their conclusions in the face of contradictory evidence or reasonable doubts.

To proceed as Spender does—that is, to invalidate a position because it relies on selected data—precludes the possibility of anyone ever reaching the truth, because all conclusions are based on selected data. Spender's approach invalidates every feminist conclusion, including her own contention that "wrong" is a "meaningless category."

Despite their rejection of objective truth, gender feminists seem to claim absolute knowledge when it comes to the evils of patriarchy and the damage that reproductive technology has done to women. In her introduction to *Reconstructing Babylon: Essays on Women and Technology*, editor Patricia Hynes presents two basic charges against reproductive technologies: (1) since they are "insufficiently" tested, they are injurious to women; and (2) they have been developed by men for use on women's bodies.

The first of these charges, insufficient testing, is not a fundamental one; by this I mean that even if the technologies were adequately tested, gender feminists would not alter their stance. The second accusation, however, is fundamental. Because reproductive technology has been developed by men, it is prima facie and axiomatically deemed to be opposed to the interests of women. Accordingly, only women who have been damaged are given a voice. The vast number of women who have been benefited are given no voice at all. If they are heard at all, it is only to dismiss or discredit them. Women who use surrogate mothers are said to be 'enslaving' the wombs of others; women who request IVF are placed on the same level as lab animals undergoing experiments.

The victims are not merely the women who have chosen such procedures but *all* women, because every woman must live in the culture created by reproductive technology. And, in case the present day is not enough to carry their argument forward, gender feminists paint an Orwellian picture of how future patriarchy might use technology. In her essay, "How the New Reproductive Technologies Will Affect All Women," Gena Corea argues that genetic manipulation will start with therapeutic purposes, for example, for the correction of gene defects such as multiple sclerosis.

Ironically, the only way to combat the possibility of such an Orwellian future is to insist upon precisely what is being denied, namely, that every woman have the absolute right to determine her own reproductive destiny. The central issue of reproductive technology is the same one that dominated the crusade for abortion rights, that is, the issue of choice, "a woman's body, a woman's right." It is the issue of individual choice.

The Attack on Women's Contracts

Gender feminists cannot escape the haunting issue of choice. There is a real tension between their claims that women must fully control their reproductive functions and that certain reproductive choices are unacceptable.

Common sense dictates that if women have the right to say no to reproductive technology, they must also have the right to say yes. Moreover, if a woman asks for a procedure, such as in vitro fertilization, pays the bill, and willingly undergoes the process, common sense seems to indicate that she has consented to that procedure. At least, this is what most people mean by the word "consent." If gender feminists wish to maintain that consent is not present, the burden of proof falls firmly on their shoulders.

By way of proof, gender feminists claim that women who use reproductive technology are not really choosing in a meaningful sense of that word. They argue that dissident feminists who point to the overwhelming evidence of such consent are ignoring the fact that women have been oppressed for centuries. The limited and negative range of alternatives that patriarchy currently allows for women cannot be called true choices.

With reference to surrogacy contracts, Janice G. Raymond castigates liberal feminists who emphasize choice. She compares them to Judge Sorkow, the judge who ruled on the surrogacy case of Baby M. Sorkow equated the right to be a surrogate with the right to have an abortion. Raymond calls this "pseudo-feminist rhetoric":

> There's a conscious manipulation of language and reality that happens when defenders of surrogacy use the rhetoric of "procreative liberty," knowing that many women will resonate with this phrase because of the feminist emphasis on reproductive choice articulated around the abortion issue.[33]

Perhaps the main vehicle by which choices are enacted in society is that of written agreements. Thus, gender feminism is waging war upon women's "wrong" contracts. As a touchstone in this crusade against contracts gender feminists have singled out surrogacy contracts. These are contracts by which fertile women "rent out" their wombs as incubators for infertile women who wish to have a child. The case against such contracts is spelled out by Phyllis Chesler in her essay, "Mothers on Trial: Custody and the 'Baby M' Case": "[A] contract that is both immoral and illegal isn't and shouldn't be enforceable.... Only a woman who, like all women, is seen as nothing but a surrogate uterus, is supposed to live up to—or be held down for—the most punitive, most dehumanizing of contracts."[34]

In general, the case against surrogacy contracts rests on three basic assertions: first, the surrogate is selling herself into a form of slavery and this is an invalid contract; second, the surrogate cannot give informed consent because she does not know how she will feel about the child she is carrying to term; and, third, such contracts are against the public good.

These objections are commonly hurled in one form or another against most types of reproductive technology.

The first objection to surrogacy contracts is that the surrogate is selling herself (or at least her womb) into slavery. But there is nothing different—in kind—from a woman renting her womb and a woman renting out other parts of her body, as a secretary, lawyer, proofreader, or chemical engineer. Since these other activities could be called slave contracts as well, the essential point becomes: What constitutes slavery?

The key aspect of slavery is the alienation of the will, that is, a person sells not only the use of his or her body but also his or her moral and legal jurisdiction over it. This is the key difference between a slave and a wage earner. A wage earner temporarily rents out an aspect of his or her body. A slave permanently sells all rights to it. In essence, the slave transfers his or her self-ownership over to another person.

Of course, a slavery contract quickly dissolves into contradictions. For example, the instant a person signs such a contract, he or she instantly loses all moral and legal responsibility for living up to its terms. After all, the person would no longer be a legal entity who needs to abide by contracts or would even be able to do so.

Thus, a slavery contract reduces itself to absurdity. In human terms, all that can be contracted out are services. In other words, no contract can involve alienating the self-ownership and the will of the contractee, for it is self-ownership that makes the contractee a legally accountable human being.

Selling oneself into slavery fails to pass muster as a contract in another essential way. As Chesley points out, everyone has the right to breach a contract and pay the penalty for doing so. But this, too, assumes a morally and legally accountable entity who can choose to break a contract and be held responsible for the consequences. The real problem with surrogacy contracts is not that they constitute slavery but that the rights being temporarily relinquished and the consequences of a breach are ill-defined.

The second reason why gender feminists object to surrogacy contracts is that the surrogate cannot give informed consent. The first thing to note about this contention is how insulting it is to all women, not merely those who are involved in surrogacy arrangements. It is just another way of saying that women do not know their own minds and cannot be trusted with control of their own bodies. Men have told women this for centuries, now gender feminists mouth the same old patriarchal line.

Part of the gender feminist objection hinges on the current vagueness of the surrogacy contract, which often does not specify the rights and duties of those involved as, for example, who will care for the baby if it is born deformed. Does the surrogate agree to a cesarean if the fetus is in danger? What remedies are available for breach of contract? Without definition of these terms, informed consent may be a problem.

But even with these questions resolved, the heart of the gender feminists' objection remains: they claim that surrogates cannot give informed consent. In this, gender feminists are ironically in agreement with that bastion of patriarchy, the court system. In ruling on the surrogacy case of Baby M (1988) the New Jersey Supreme Court deemed that there was a lack of informed consent, because the surrogate did not know how she would feel about the baby until it was born.

A similar statement could be made about almost every contract. If I sell my family home, for example, I do not know how much I will miss the memories it holds until I no longer have the house. Or if I contract to produce paintings, I do not know how emotionally connected I will feel to my works until they are executed and sold. Equally, if I agree to mow someone's lawn on Saturday afternoon, I do not know how personally important that free time might be to me until Saturday rolls around. To say that I am able to breach a contract, with impunity, simply because I have second thoughts is in essence to say that no contract exists at all.

Lack of consent is sometimes said to exist because the surrogate is compelled by the threat of a lawsuit into complying with the surrogacy contract. But this aspect of a written agreement is almost a definition of what constitutes a contract, namely, it is an agreement that leaves a person vulnerable to a legal remedy if breached. To say that this factor constitutes coercion is to say that contracts, in and of themselves, are coercive.

This, in turn, eliminates the very distinction between a peaceful and a forced exchange: a contract is nothing more than the recording of a peaceful exchange of goods and/or services. The fact that one or both of the parties might really need, for example, the money involved in no way admits an element of force into the arrangement. After all, it is assumed from the beginning that both parties want or need what is being exchanged. That is precisely why the exchange is occurring. The more desperately someone needs the exchange, the more they stand to benefit from it. The terms of the contract may reflect this desperation (e.g., high interest rates, low wages), but this is a result of a bad bargaining position, not of force. Presumably, once the exchange has taken place, the need is reduced and future bargaining positions will be improved.

As for who controls the transaction, a surrogate (or any woman) can have no greater control than the right to say yes or no to the terms of a contract and to have her voice taken seriously in a court of law.

Contracts as a Violation of the Public Good. Gender feminists raise yet another objection against surrogate contracts, namely, that they violate the public good. They create a class of women who can be bought as breeders and, in the process, be stripped of dignity. This strips all women of dignity. In testifying before the House Judiciary Committee of the State of Michigan in October 1987, Janice G. Raymond declared:

> I am here today to testify against this bill that attempts to regulate surrogacy.... My position is that surrogate contracts should be made unenforceable as a matter of public policy, and that they reinforce the subordination of women by making women into reproductive objects and reproductive commodities.[35]

In a revealing statement, Raymond claimed that women have no real right to do anything that damages their dignity—presumably, as defined by gender feminist standards. Raymond contended: "A surrogate arrangement offers no dignity to women and therefore cannot be called a real right. It violates the core of human dignity to hire a woman's body for the breeding of a child so that someone else's genes can be perpetuated."[36]

Yet, elsewhere Raymond admits that, under certain circumstances, surrogacy can be a valid experience, much like donating an organ to a sibling: "Many, for example, feel an obligation to donate bone marrow in response to a family member's need. This kind of limited individual situation gets expanded to a social level, however, when a giving population has been socialized to give as part of their role."[37]

The statement is revealing. Most gender feminists do not attack women who bear a child on behalf of an infertile relative, such as a sister. Yet this, too, is the medicalization of childbirth. They do not attack women who compassionately "loan out" their wombs, but only those who commercially "rent out" the same service. In other words, gender feminists are condemning not reproductive technology, but the commercialization of reproduction. This leads us to the institution that many gender feminists see as the evil hand behind reproductive technology, the free market.

Demonizing the Free Market

In her essay, "Commercial Surrogacy," Linda M. Whiteford sketches the rationale behind rejecting the "money motive" in surrogacy:

> Commercial surrogacy exploits socioeconomic class differences, using financial need and emotional need as currency. The exchange of money transforms surrogacy from an altruistic gift between sisters or friends into baby selling or womb renting and powerfully affects social relationships.[38]

According to Whiteford, the profit motive is what maintains socioeconomic injustice:

> The exchange of money for surrogacy codifies power and class inequities between those who can afford to buy new life and those who sell their ability to create life. The exchanges of money for surrogacy categorizes people as buyers and sellers, categories based on socioeconomic differences.[39]

In other words, the fact that someone (a surrogate) truly needs money invalidates her contracts on the grounds of socioeconomic coercion. But it is precisely those who need money who most need the right to contract for it. To tell poor women that they have no right to sell their services—whether as a waitress, a nurse, or a surrogate—deals a death blow to their economic self-determination. Their services may be the only thing they have to leverage themselves out of poverty. They need the right to contract far more than the rich and powerful do.

Yet Paula A. Treichler captures the repugnance with which gender feminists respond to contracts and the other trappings of a free market: "Certainly the language of the marketplace pervades discussions of childbearing even among those to whom the market approach is repugnant."[40] This attack on the free market assumes that profit makers are indifferent or inimical to the interests of the women who are actual or potential customers. Yet, in a competitive marketplace, the only way to maximize profits is to cater to those who desire a product or service.

The free market has no mechanism to force anyone to provide or consume a service. Nor can the free market impose any form of morality. All it does is reflect and satisfy the preferences of the individuals who make up society. To the extent that the free market has one, its underlying ideology is that every human being has the right to act as his or her own agent in exchanging property and services. The free market assumes that individuals are self owners with property rights. In other words, "a woman's body, a woman's right."

Indeed, a true gender feminist should argue for the greater commercialization of reproductive technology. Because this is nothing less than a woman's right to use and dispose of her own body in a manner that profits her, whether that profit is monetary or takes the form of an infant in a mother's arms.

The hostility of gender feminists toward individual choice and their insistence on class rights has led them to reject the free market. Instead, they turn to the government for justice. Many people have commented on the irony of this. After all, throughout the centuries it has been government that has persecuted women. It burned them as witches; it dictated they could not own property; it banned information on birth control; it committed healthy girls to insane asylums; it condoned domestic violence; it banned women from universities. Government, not the free market, has thoroughly proven itself to be the enemy of women.

Conclusion

With their collectivist agenda, gender feminists have harmed the drive to preserve abortion rights. By attacking reproductive technology, they have hindered the prochoice movement in several ways:

1. Their arguments against reproductive technology apply with equal force to abortion. For example, the contention that all modern medical techniques are the creations of patriarchy leaves little doubt as to where abortion stands.

2. Gender feminists have splintered the movement and made a concerted effort against the prolife movement unlikely.

3. Gender feminists have essentially joined hands with the religious right in an attack on, for example, surrogate motherhood. This unholy alliance only strengthens those who oppose abortion rights.

4. Gender feminists have so muddied the issue of abortion that it can no longer command a clear focus and become the rallying point that it was in the '60s.

Gender feminists are now at odds with liberal feminists, who are puzzled by the claim that procedures that seem to increase the choices of women are declared forms of oppression. Liberal feminists remember too well how birth control and abortion—whatever their flaws and abuses—liberated vast numbers of women from the tyranny of involuntary motherhood. They find it difficult to view such salvation as merely another fraud perpetuated by white male culture.

The debate about reproductive technology is about choice. Prochoice feminists seek to expand the alternatives for women, including procedures such as in vitro fertilization. Gender feminists seek to narrow alternatives by eliminating the unacceptable ones, that is, the ones provided by patriarchy. Nothing less than the principle of "a woman's body, a woman's right" is at stake. If it is lost, what remains?

Notes

1. Patricia Spallone and Deborah Lynn Steinberg, eds., *Made to Order: The Myth of Reproductive and Genetic Progress* (Oxford: Pergamon Press, 1987), p. 13.
2. Ibid., p. 4.
3. Heather Menzies, "In His Image: Science and Technology," in *Twist and Shout: A Decade of Feminist Writings in This Magazine*, ed., Susan Crean (Toronto: Second Story Press, 1992), pp. 157–158.
4. Catharine MacKinnon, "Liberalism and the Death of Feminism," in *Sexual Liberals and the Attack on Feminism*, pp. 6–7.
5. Ibid.
6. Twiss Butler, "Abortion and Pornography," in *Sexual Liberals and the Attack on Feminism*, p. 117.
7. Ibid.
8. Andrea Dworkin, "Woman Hating Right and Left," in *Sexual Liberals and the Attack on Feminism*, p. 29.
9. Ibid.
10. Barbara Katz Rothman, "The Meaning of Choice in Reproductive Technology," in *Test Tube Women: What Future for Motherhood?* (London: Pandora Press, 1989), p. 23.
11. Elayne Rapping, "The Future of Motherhood," in *Women, Class, and the Feminist Imagination: A Socialist-Feminist Reader*, ed. Karen V. Hansen and Ilene J. Philipson (Philadelphia: Temple University Press, 1990), p. 543.
12. As quoted in "Fetal Rights and the New Eugenics," *Science for the People* March/April 1984, p. 27.
13. Ibid.
14. Margery Shaw, "The Potential Plaintiff: Preconception and Prenatal Torts," in *Genetics and the Law, II* (New York: Plenum Press, 1980), p. 228.

15. Gena Corea, "The New Reproductive Technologies" pp. 85, 87, 89.

16. Paula A. Treichler, "Feminism, Medicine, and the Meaning of Childbirth," in *Body/Politics: Women and the Discourses of Science* ed. Mary Jacobus, Evelyn Fox Keller, and Sally Shuttleworth (New York: Routledge, 1990), pp. 120–121.

17. *Australian Left Review* 89:46–55

18. Gena Corea "How the New Reproductive Technologies Will Affect All Women," p. 41.

19. Patricia Hynes, ed., *Reconstructing Babylon: Essays on Women and Technology* (Indiana University Press, Bloomington, 1991), p. 57.

20. Janice G. Raymond, "Fetalists and Feminists: They Are Not the Same," in *Made to Order*, p. 62.

21. Elisabeth Beck-Gernsheim, "From the Pill to Test-Tube Babies," in *Healing Technology: Feminist Perspectives* ed. Kathryn Strother Ratcliff (Ann Arbor: University of Michigan Press, 1989), p. 26.

22. Ibid., p. 30.

23. Prologue to *Made to Order*, p. 7.

24. Ibid., p. 41.

25. Ibid., p. 56.

26. Ibid.

27. Lynne C. Garner and Richard C. Tessler, "Technology in Childbirth: Effects on Postpartum Moods," in *Healing Technology*, p. 194.

28. As quoted in *Imprimus* (Hillsdale College, June 1990).

29. Samuel C. Florman, *Blaming Technology: The Irrational Search for Scapegoats* (New York: St. Martin's Press, 1981), p. 125.

30. Ibid.

31. Dale Spender, "Theorizing About Theorizing," in *Body/Politics*, p. 28.

32. Ibid.

33. Janice G. Raymond, "Sexual and Reproductive Liberalism," in *Sexual Liberals and the Attack on Feminism*, p. 111.

34. Phyllis Chesler, "Mothers on Trial: Custody and the 'Baby M' Case," in *Sexual Liberals and the Attack on Feminism*, p. 101.

35. Janice G. Raymond "Sexual and Reproductive Liberalism," in *Sexual Liberals and the Attack on Feminism*, p. 137.

36. Ibid.

37. Janice G. Raymond, "Of Eggs, Embryos, and Altruism," in *Sexual Liberals and the Attack on Feminism*, p. 67.

38. Linda M. Whiteford, "Commercial Surrogacy," in *New Approaches to Human Reproduction: Social and Ethical Dimensions*, ed. Linda M. Whiteford and Marilyn L. Poland (Boulder: Westview Press, 1989), p. 149.

39. Ibid.

40. Paula A. Treichler, "Feminism, Medicine, and the Meaning of Childbirth," in *Body/Politics*, p. 114.

CHAPTER TWELVE

A Brief
Bibliographical Essay

Sexual correctness is a dogma that permits no dissent. Gender feminists have no scruples about silencing and dismissing the voices of women who disagree. Thus, though individualist feminism is a rich tradition with deep roots in American history, it is virtually ignored. This bibliographical essay is a step toward reclaiming an aspect of feminist history that the orthodoxy would rather relegate to the dust bin.

Today, the majority of American women feel alienated from forms of feminism that do not address their daily needs. One can understand their disillusionment. American feminism has forgotten its roots and has taken a disastrous turn away from the true interests of women. It is time to rediscover the rich and distinctly American tradition of individualist feminism, a tradition based on the principles of self-ownership and equal treatment under just laws. Although the American tradition draws heavily upon British classical liberalism—especially the work of British feminist Mary Wollstonecraft—Americans organized around issues uniquely their own, such as Puritanism, the American Revolution, and slavery.

As an organized and self-conscious movement, American feminism arosein the 1830s. Earlier, women who made a stand for their own conscience against authority did so as individuals. Anne Marbury Hutchinson (1591–1643) led the first organized attack on the Puritan orthodoxy of the Massachusetts Bay Colony, thus evoking the sexual equality practiced by some European Protestant sects. *The Antinomian Controversy 1636–1638: A Documentary History* (1968; Durham: Duke University Press, 1990), edited by David D. Hall, is an excellent collection of contemporaneous documents surrounding Hutchinson's trial and banishment. Selma R. Williams's *Divine Rebel: The Life of Anne Marbury Hutchinson* (New York: Holt, Rinehart & Wilson, 1981) is a good biography.

Abigail Adams (1744–1818), wife of John Adams, had a genius for letter writing. Her correspondence is replete with praise for the competence of her sex and with condemnations of slavery on the grounds that all human beings have equal rights. Indeed, Page Smith in his two-volume *John Adams* (Garden City, N.Y.: Doubleday 1962) considered Abigail to be a full partner in her husband's career. Most of Abigail Adams's surviving correspondence is in the Adams Papers, Massachusetts Historical Society. A good selection of her letters can be found in *The Adams— Jefferson Letters: The Complete Correspondence Between Thomas Jefferson and Abigail and John Adams* (Chapel Hill: University of North Carolina Press, c. 1959) edited by Lester J. Capon.

Mercy Otis Warren (1728–1814) was the most prolific "woman of the American revolution," with works that viewed history and politics as a struggle between liberty and power. Between 1772 and 1805, Warren published five plays, three political satires, three books of poetry, a pamphlet critiquing the recently proposed Constitution, and one of the most important histories of the American Revolution. Much of her literary work appeared in *Poems: Dramatic and Miscellaneous* (1790). Her satirical play, *The Adulateur*, first appeared anonymously in the Boston newspaper, the *Massachusetts Spy* (1772; pamphlet, Boston, 1773). This work portrayed Thomas Hutchinson, the royal governor of Massachusetts as the character Rapatio, a ruler who sought to crush the love of liberty. Her next play, *The Defeat* (1773), again featured Rapatio. *The Group* (1775) satirized the Massachusetts Tories under such evil names as Judge Meager. These satires are available in *Plays and Poems of Mercy Otis Warren: Facsimile Reproductions Compiled and with an Introduction by Benjamin Franklin* (Delmar, N.Y.: Scholars' Facsimiles and Reprints, 1980).

Warren's major work, *History of the Rise, Progress, and Termination of the American Revolution, Interspersed with Biographical, Political, and Moral Observations* (Boston: Manning and Loring, 1805; Liberty Classics, Indianapolis, 1988), is one of the most important contemporaneous histories of the period. The largest body of Warren's manuscript material rests with the Massachusetts Historical Society. Mary Elizabeth Regan's *Pundit and Prophet of the Old Republic: The Life and Times of Mercy Otis Warren* (Ph.D. diss., University of California, 1984) provides good biographical material. Linda Kerber's overview, *Women of the Republic: Intellect and Ideology in Revolutionary America* (Chapel Hill: University of North Carolina Press, 1980), is valuable for a more general understanding of women's role in the American Revolution.

In the 1820s, Frances Wright, a follower of the Utopian philosopher Robert Owen, visited America and wrote a long series of letters home to

Glasgow. These formed the well-received travel memoir *Views of Society and Manners in America* (1821; Cambridge, Mass.: Belknap Press, 1963; edited by Paul R. Baker). Written from a libertarian and secular point of view, this book used American society to critique oppressive conditions in Europe. Returning to America, Wright championed the antislavery cause and that of the Utopian communities, serving as coeditor of the *New Harmony Gazette*, which subsequently became the *Free Enquirer* (New York, 1829).

In 1828 Wright created a sensation by becoming the first woman to make a lecture tour of America. She demanded legal rights for married women, liberal divorce laws, and birth control. A recent source of biographical data is *Frances Wright: Rebel in America* (Cambridge, Mass.: Harvard University Press, 1984) by Celia Morris. Some of Wright's speeches are reprinted in *Course of Popular Lectures* (1829; expanded edition 1836). Wright's letters are scattered in various collections, but files of the *Free Enquirer* (for the period of her editorship) are at Rutgers University and Cornell.

In the 1830s a feminist movement grew from the ranks of abolitionism, a movement that demanded the immediate cessation of slavery on the grounds that every man is a self-owner. Many abolitionists were Quakers, reared in the tenet of sexual equality and with a tradition of female ministry. Inevitably, abolitionist women asked: "Do not we own ourselves as well?" This was the birth of individualist feminism. And it was expressed largely through lectures, pamphlets, and articles that appeared in periodicals, especially *The Liberator* (Boston, 1831–1865, edited by William Lloyd Garrison), available on microfilm from the Massachusetts Historical Society.

Sarah Moore Grimke (1792–1873), an abolitionist Quaker from South Carolina, shot one of the first feminist arrows in her essay *Letters on the Equality of the Sexes and the Condition of Woman, Addressed to Mary Parker, President of the Boston Female Anti-Slavery Society* (Boston: Isaac Knapp, 1838), drawing a parallel between the legal status of slaves and of women. Sarah's sister, Angelina Emily Grimke (1805–1879) published a series of letters in the *Liberator* (1838), which later became the influential pamphlet *Letters to Catherine Beecher in Reply to an Essay on Slavery and Abolitionism* (Boston: Isaac Knapp, 1838). Two of these letters defended the rights of women as citizens and human beings.

Much of the Grimkes' impact came from the fact that they, as women, broke convention by publicly speaking out. On February 21, 1838, for example, Angelina Grimke spoke before a committee of the legislature of the state of Massachusetts, thus becoming the first American woman to address a legislative body. The text was reprinted in *The Liberator* (May 2, 1838).

The Grimkes' key works and speeches have been reprinted in *The Public Years of Sarah and Angelina Grimke: Selected Writings, 1835–1839* (Columbia University Press, 1989). The definitive biography is Gerda Lerner's *The Grimke Sisters from South Carolina: Rebels Against Slavery* (1967; New York: Schocken Books, 1971). However, *The Grimke Sisters: Sarah and Angelina Grimke, The First Women Advocates of Abolition and Woman's Rights* (Boston: Lee and Sheppard, 1885; Greenwood Press, 1969) by Catharine Birney is of interest because Birney was a personal friend who used diaries and letters from the Grimkes as source material. The primary manuscript source is the Theodore Dwight Weld Collection, William L. Clements Library, The University of Michigan, Ann Arbor.

In 1848 the venerable abolitionist Quaker, Lucretia Coffin Mott (1793–1880) helped to organize the Seneca Falls Convention, the first women's rights conference. She delivered the opening and closing addresses. In *Discourse on Woman* (1850) Mott attributed the alleged inferiority of women to the oppression they had suffered. *Lucretia Mott: Her Complete Speeches and Sermons* (edited by Dana Greene, New York: Edwin Mellen Press, 1980) is an excellent collection of her work. The most satisfying biography remains Otelia Cromwell's *Lucretia Mott* (New York: Russell & Russell, 1958). Margaret Hope Bacon's more recent biography *Valiant Friend: The Life of Lucretia Mott* (New York: Walker, 1980) also provides valuable background material.

Lydia Maria Child (1802–1880) was probably the most popular American woman writer of her day, publishing more than 40 works, from children's stories to abolitionist pamphlets to biographies of Madame de Staël and Madame Roland. Her two-volume *History of the Condition of Women, in Various Ages and Nations* (1835; New York: C. S. Francis, 1845) sketched the debased status of women throughout history in an informative, but sometimes inaccurate, manner. In this work, Child avoided offending her audience by only indirectly addressing feminist issues. *Letters by Lydia Maria Child* (1882) contains selected correspondence and a biographical introduction by John G. Whittier. A recent and excellent biography is Deborah Pickman Clifford's *Crusader for Freedom: A Life of Lydia Maria Child* (Boston: Beacon Press, 1992). Cornell University has the largest collection of Child's papers.

Maria Weston Chapman (1806–1885) helped to transmit British classical liberalism to the United States through her two-volume *Harriet Martineau's Autobiography* (J. R. Osgood, 1877; Boston: Houghton, Mifflin, 1877). Chapman appended some 460 pages of tribute and reminiscence. The reprint (Farnborough: Hants; England 1969) omits the memorials.

The scope of contributions from other abolitionist women, such as

Abbie Kelley Foster, Lydia White, Prudence Crandell, and Lucy Stone, precludes mention. Indeed, an exhaustive survey would include Harriet Beecher Stowe's (1811–1896) *Uncle Tom's Cabin, or, Life Among the Lowly* (1851; New York: Viking 1982); in the preface to the 1878 edition, Stowe confessed to keeping an abolitionist text by Angelina Grimke's husband in her workbasket by day and under her pillow at night for inspiration. Also, two essays defending women in William Graham Sumner's *War and Other Essays* (edited by Albert G. Keller; New Haven: Yale University Press, 1919) were undoubtedly influenced by his experience with abolitionist women.

Overviews of this key period for individualist feminism can be found in *Radical Abolitionism: Anarchism and the Government of God in Antislavery Thought* (Ithaca: Cornell University Press, 1973) by Lewis Perry and in Blanche Glassman Hersh's *The Slavery of Sex: Feminist Abolitionists in America* (Urbana: University of Illinois Press, 1978).

Meanwhile, another tradition provided a vehicle for individualistic women: transcendentalism. This philosophy was rooted in natural law and a belief in the perfectibility of human beings. Margaret Fuller (1810–1850), who had studied the works of John Locke with Lydia Maria Child, came under the influence of the transcendentalists Ralph Waldo Emerson and Bronson Alcott. Fuller began to publish in the *Dial* (Boston, 1840–1844), the periodical of the Club of Transcendentalists. Indeed, between 1840 and 1842, Fuller acted as editor. Her book, *Woman in the Nineteenth Century* (1845; New York: Norton, 1971), grew from an essay in the *Dial* and presaged the concept of sisterhood. The book has become an American classic.

Fuller also worked as a literary critic for the *New York Tribune*; many of her articles were collected in *Papers on Literature and Art* (New York: Wiley & Putnam, 1846). *Memoirs of Margaret Fuller Ossoli* (2 vols., 1852; New York: Burt Franklin, 1972), edited by Ralph Waldo Emerson, William H. Channing, and James Freeman Clarke, provides excellent background material. Mason Wade's *Margaret Fuller: Whetstone of Genius* (New York: Viking, 1940) provides valuable biographical data. *The Woman and the Myth: Margaret Fuller's Life and Writing* (Old Westbury, N.Y.: The Feminist Press, 1976) by Bell Gale Chevigny mixes biography with reprints of Fuller's material. The range of her work is well represented in *The Writings of Margaret Fuller*, edited by Mason Wade (New York: Viking, 1941), which includes a full listing of periodical contributions. *The Essential Margaret Fuller* (New Brunswick, N.J.: Rutgers, 1992), edited by Jeffrey Steele, is also valuable.

Elizabeth Palmer Peabody's (1804–1894) *Record of a School* (1835;

New York: Arno Press 1969) presented a transcendentalist view of moral education and established Bronson Alcott (the focus of her report) as an important figure in intellectual circles. In May 1849 the single issue of her own transcendentalist periodical *Aesthetic Papers* introduced Henry David Thoreau's *Civil Disobedience*. *Last Evening with Allston and Other Papers* (1886; AMS Press, 1975) collects her essays from the *Dial* and *Aesthetic Papers* along with later pieces.

Between 1861 and 1865 the Civil War absorbed the energy of feminists, who put social causes aside to work for the war effort. Afterward, many women joined a mainstream campaign to make the rights of women part of the U.S. Constitution. Individualist feminism became splintered, finding expression in radical periodicals, especially those championing free thought, utopian communities, and free love. The free thought movement denied that the church had any authority to regulate individuals. The best source for women in the free thought movement is George A. MacDonald's two-volume *50 Years of Free Thought* (New York: Truthseeker, 1929, 1931), which centered around the periodical the *Truthseeker* (1873–present). Raymond Lee Muncey's *Sex and Marriage in Utopian Communities: Nineteenth-Century America* (Bloomington: Indiana University Press, 1973) provides a good general overview of feminism within utopian communities.

The most important vehicle for individualist feminism was the free love movement, which declared all sexual matters to be the province of the individuals involved, not of government. The most important free love periodical was *Lucifer the Light Bearer* (Valley Falls, Kansas 1883–1890; Topeka 1890–1896; Chicago 1896–1907), edited by Moses Harman. *Lucifer* succeeded the *Valley Falls Liberal* (1880), which began with no formal editors; it was, in turn, succeeded by *The American Journal of Eugenics* (1907–1910), edited by Moses Harman. *Lucifer* had a policy of publishing frank letters without editing language (e.g., one letter argued that forced sex within marriage was rape). This policy caused Harman to be convicted three times under the Comstock Laws of 1873. His final imprisonment occurred when he was seventy-five years old. During these confinements Lillian Harman, Lillie D. White, and Lois Waisbrooker assumed editorship. Many individualist feminists, such as Celia B. Whitehead, Lillie D. White, and Lois Waisbrooker published in *Lucifer*.

Lucifer and its staff produced many pamphlets. Moses Harman's include: *Love in Freedom* (Chicago, 1900); *Institutional Marriage* (Chicago, 1901); *A Free Man's Creed: Discussion of Love in Freedom as Opposed to Institutional Marriage* (Los Angeles, 1908). At the age of sixteen, Lillian Harman, Moses' daughter, was imprisoned for marrying fellow free-lover E. C. Walker without state or church sanction. Lillian's pamphlets include *Marriage and Morality* (pamphlet, Chicago: Light Bearer Library, 1900); *Some Problems of Social Freedom* (London, 1898).

Eventually, Lillian Harman and E. C. Walker broke from *Lucifer* and published their own free love periodical *Fair Play* (1888–1891), first from Valley Falls, Kansas, and then from Sioux City, Iowa.

The Kansas State Historical Society in Topeka has a run of *Lucifer* and most other Kansas free love periodicals, as well as many pamphlets. The Labadie Collection, University of Michigan, Ann Arbor, contains some of the Harman papers. The best secondary source on this radical circle remains Hal D. Sears's *The Sex Radicals: Free Love in High Victorian America* (Lawrence, Kansas: Regents Press, 1977).

The Word, subtitled *A Monthly Journal of Reform* (Princeton and Cambridge, Mass.: 1872–1890, 1892–1893) and edited by Ezra Heywood, began as a labor paper, but came to focus more and more on free love issues such as birth control. Elizabeth Cady Stanton was among its many female contributors. *The Word* also sparked pamphlets. Ezra Heywood's essay on birth control, *Cupid's Yokes: The Binding Forces of Conjugal Life: An Essay to Consider Some Moral and Physiological Phases of Love and Marriage, Wherein Is Asserted the Natural Right and Necessity of Sexual Self-Government* (Princeton, Mass., 1876), was the most controversial pamphlet in the history of individualist feminism. Its distribution, estimated at 50,000 to 200,000, contravened the Comstock Laws, which outlawed birth control information as obscene. Heywood was imprisoned repeatedly.

Uncivil Liberties (1873) was also written by Ezra Heywood with his wife Angela's input. The pamphlet called for woman suffrage on the grounds that it would socially emancipate both sexes. Many of Heywood's essays can be found in *The Collected Works of Ezra H. Heywood* (Weston, Mass.: M & S Press, 1985). A microfilm run of *The Word* is available from the Massachusetts Historical Society and contains such gems as Angela Heywood's defense of abortion based on the idea of "a woman's body, a woman's right," perhaps the first such defense in American feminism. *The Word* also published Walt Whitman who, as a child, attended lectures by Frances Wright. After Whitman's book *Leaves of Grass* was threatened by the Comstock Laws, *The Word* (1882) boldly reprinted two of its poems, "To a Common Prostitute" and "A Woman Waits for Me."

No less controversial, but less substantial, was *Woodhull and Claflin's Weekly* (1870–1876), edited by Victoria Woodhull (1838–1927) and her sister Tennessee Claflin (1845–1923). Woodhull was a free love, free speech radical whose pamphlets were said to be written by others, especially by the libertarian Stephen Pearl Andrews and by Woodhull's husband, Colonel Blood. Her radical views on marriage were aired in the pamphlet *Tried As By Fire* (published lecture, 1874). *The Victoria Woodhull Reader* (Weston, Mass.: M & S Press, 1974), edited by Madeleine B. Stern, is the best source for Woodhull's original work. Emanie Sachs's biography *"The Terrible Siren": Victoria Woodhull, (1838–1927)* (New York: Harper, 1928; Arno Press) is the most valuable source of biographical material.

The individualist anarchist periodical *Liberty* subtitled *Not the Daughter But the Mother of Order* (Boston, Mass., 1881–1907), edited by Benjamin R. Tucker, was another platform for women. Its contributors comprise a virtual honor roll of individualist feminists: Gertrude Kelly, Bertha Marvin, Lillian Harman, Clara Dixon Davidson, Ellen Battelle Dietrick, Kate Field, Emma Schumm, Juliet Severance, Charlotte Perkins Stetson, Josephine Tilton, Helen Tufts, and Lois Waisbrooker. Unfortunately, most of the subjects discussed had only implied importance for women.

Stephen Pearl Andrews (1812–1886), a coeditor of *Liberty*, published the booklet *Love, Marriage, and Divorce and the Sovereignty of the Individual* (1853; Weston, Mass.: M & S Press, 1975). This was an exchange of sorts between Horace Greeley and Andrews. The fundamental difference between them concerned an individual's relationship with government. Andrews believed that individuals could and should govern themselves. He also suggested the superiority of women. Charles Shively's *The Thought of Stephen Pearl Andrews, 1812–1886* (master's thesis, University of Wisconsin, 1960) deals with Andrews's views of sex, marriage, and the family.

Meanwhile, perhaps the most important theorist in individualist feminism worked in relative isolation: Voltairine de Cleyre (1866–1912). This poet-anarchist, named after Voltaire, is best remembered for her essay *Anarchism and American Traditions*, in which she argued that anarchism was the logical consequence of the principles of the American Revolution. De Cleyre's anarchism had the same root as her passion for women's rights, the hatred of tyranny.

The best source for de Cleyre's writing is *Selected Works of Voltairine de Cleyre*, edited by Alexander Berkman, with a biographical sketch by Hippolyte Havel (1914; New York: Source Book Press, 1972.) The definitive biography is *An American Anarchist: The Life of Voltairine de Cleyre* by Paul Avrich (Princeton, N.J.: Princeton University Press, 1978).

The turn of the century brought a pervasive repression of sexuality. After the assassination of McKinley, political radicalism was persecuted as well. Individualist feminism, which drew lifeblood from free love and individualist anarchism, died. When it was resurrected, the voices were isolated and altered.

Individualist feminism changed in another manner as well. Twentieth-century advocates generally expressed a view of economics that was different from that of their nineteenth-century counterparts. Nineteenth-century individualists had accepted a labor theory of value. Although they championed the free market, they opposed capitalism as a distortion of the marketplace. By contrast, twentieth-century individualist feminism abandoned the labor theory of value and tended to incorporate a defense of capitalism.

In 1926 *Concerning Women* (New York: Arno Press, 1972) by Suzanne La Follette became the first book-length treatment of individualist feminism. La Follette transmitted individualist feminism into a new century. Her defense of the free market led her to vigorously oppose state intrusion into women's lives, such as protective labor and minimum wage laws. As a journalist, La Follette worked with her mentor Albert Jay Nock on both *The Nation* and *The Freeman*.

Although Emma Goldman was a communist, her two books *My Disillusionment in Russia* and *My Further Disillusionment in Russia* (Garden City, N.Y.: Doubleday Page, 1923, 1924), contributed to individualism by attacking the Russian social experiment. *Give Me Liberty* (1936) by Rose Wilder Lane (1886–1968), one of the most influential women of her day, was written in the same vein. This booklet charted Lane's progress from socialism to libertarianism as a result of directly experiencing life under socialist regimes. Published during the Great Depression by the *Saturday Evening Post*, it warned against the state socialism inherent in Roosevelt's New Deal. A consistent critic of Roosevelt, Lane withdrew to her farm in Connecticut where she refused to participate in social security or to earn enough to pay taxes. Lane's most famous work, *The Discovery of Freedom: Man's Struggle Against Authority* (1943; New York: Arno Press, 1972), is an overview of mankind's intellectual progress through history. It attempts to explain the struggle between freedom and authority.

The Lady and the Tycoon (Caldwell, Ohio: Caxton, 1972), edited by Roger Lea MacBride, provides a portion of Lane's correspondence. An interesting exchange of correspondence is captured in *Dorothy Thompson and Rose Wilder Lane: Forty Years of Friendship, 1921–1960* (Columbia: University of Missouri Press, 1991), edited by William Holtz. The best biographical source is *Rose Wilder Lane: Her Story* (Madison Books, 1980). Some of Lane's papers are available at the Herbert Hoover Presidential Library in West Branch, Iowa.

The successful novelist Isabel Paterson also added her voice to the defense of capitalism in her nonfiction work *The God of the Machine* (1943; Caldwell, Idaho: Caxton, 1964).

Aside from individuals, two traditions also carried on the threads of individualist feminism:

1. The School of Living called for decentralization, self-sufficiency, and for replacing government action with individual initiative. This philosophy drew on the ideas of nineteenth-century individualists Henry George, Josiah Warren, Ezra Heywood, and William B. Greene. Mildred J. Loomis's *Decentralism: Where It Came From; Where Is It Going?* (The School of Living Press, 1980) has been republished under the title *Alternative Americas* (New York: Universe Books, 1982); it sets out the basics of this tradition.

2. Christian pacifism is expressed in the periodical the *Catholic Worker* (1933–present), perhaps the most widely circulated of all libertarian newspapers. Even the FBI was hard-pressed to classify the *Catholic Worker*'s brand of subversion: it opposed communism and capitalism while supporting private property and decentralization. Followers often called themselves anarchists, yet respected the authority of the church. Radical Christian pacifism places the duty to conscience above any duty to the state.

In her autobiography *The Long Loneliness* (New York: Harper & Row, 1952), Dorothy Day (1897–1980), the founder of *The Catholic Worker*, gives a sense of the philosophy and history behind this movement. Also valuable is *Dorothy Day and the Catholic Worker: A Bibliography and Index* (New York: Garland, 1986) by Anne Klejment.

Then, in the '50s and '60s Ayn Rand burst onto the intellectual scene with the philosophy of objectivism, which she expressed both in fiction and nonfiction works. Her first published work, a novelette, set the tone for the rest of her career. *Anthem* (1938; New York: New American Library, 1946) is the futuristic story of a man who rediscovers individualism in a society of absolute collectivism. Her two subsequent novels *We the Living* (1936; New York: Random, 1959) and *The Fountainhead* (1943; New York: New American Library, 1952) continue this theme of rational egoism confronted by collectivization. Rand's most famous novel, *Atlas Shrugged* (1957; New York: Random House, 1959), chronicles the breakdown of society as rational egoists resist collectivization by going "on strike."

The themes dramatized in Rand's fiction become explicit ideas in her nonfiction works. The titles of two of her nonfiction works are self-explanatory: *Capitalism: The Unknown Ideal* (New York: New American

Library, 1966) and *The Virtue of Selfishness: A New Concept of Egoism* (New York: New American Library, 1964).

Who Is Ayn Rand (1962; New York: Paperback Library, 1964) by Nathaniel Branden and Barbara Branden provides a sense of Rand's circle and its tendency to idolize her. Essays analyze the many facets of Rand and her impact. The definitive biography is Barbara Branden's *The Passion of Ayn Rand* (Garden City, N.Y.: Doubleday, 1986).

Ayn Rand built an interdisciplinary system that carried the defense of individualism and capitalism to sophisticated heights. It is surprising that her works have not ushered in a renaissance of individualist feminism. But the movement only edges toward cohesion.

The novels of objectivist Kay Nolte Smith, such as *In the Eye of the Wind* (New York: Random House, 1991), have provided a continuing voice. In 1982 a Cato anthology *Freedom, Feminism, and the State* (revised, New York: Holmes and Meier, 1991), edited by Wendy McElroy, provided a much needed overview of the background of individualist feminism. The Cato Institute has also provided a series of valuable policy studies, such as Jennifer Roback's *A Skeptical Feminist Looks at Comparable Worth* (8 Cato Policy Report 6, 7, [1986]).

A gust of fresh air swept through individualist feminism with *Sexual Personae: Art and Decadence from Nefertiti to Emily Dickinson* (New Haven: Yale University Press, 1990; New York: Vintage, 1991) by the libertarian Camille Paglia. This politically incorrect view of the role of sex within Western culture made the feminist orthodoxy howl. *Sex, Art, and American Culture* (New York: Vintage Books, 1992) caused controversy by refusing to define women as victims. That same year, 1992, also saw the publication of Joan Kennedy Taylor's excellent *Reclaiming the Mainstream: Individualist Feminism Rediscovered* (Buffalo, N.Y.: Prometheus Books, 1992), which ably charts the truest course for American feminism: individualism.

Perhaps the renaissance is at hand.

Works Cited

Works cited in the Brief Bibliographical Essay are not included here

Abbott, Michael G., ed. *Pay Equity: Means and Ends.* Kingston, Ontario: Joh Deutsch Institute, 1991.

Acker, Joan. *Doing Comparable Worth: Gender, Class, and Pay Equity.* Philadelphia: Temple University Press, 1989.

Adler, Zsuzsanna. *Rape on Trial.* London: Routledge & Kegan Paul, 1987.

Almodovar, Norma Jean. *Cop to Call Girl.* New York: Simon & Schuster, 1993.

America's Working Women: *A Documentary History, 1600 to the Present.* New York: Vintage Books, 1976.

Amir, Menachem. *Patterns in Forcible Rape.* Chicago: University of Chicago Press, 1971.

Anthony, Susan B., Elizabeth Cady Stanton, and Ida H. Harper. *The History of Woman Suffrage, vol. 1.* New York: Fowler & Wells, 1881–1922.

Arditti, Rita, ed. *Test Tube Women: What Future for Motherhood?* London: Pandora Press, 1989.

Barry, Kathleen. *Female Sexual Slavery.* New York: Avon, 1981.

Bauer, R. A., ed. *Social Indicators.* Cambridge, Mass.: MIT Press, 1966.

Becker, Gary S. *The Economics of Discrimination.* Chicago: University of Chicago Press, 1971.

Bell, Laurie, ed. *Good Girls, Bad Girls: Sex Trade Workers and Feminists Face to Face.* Toronto: Women's Press, 1987.

Blaxall, Martha and Barbara Reagan, eds. *Women and the Workplace: The Implications of Occupational Segregation.* Chicago: University of Chicago Press, 1976.

Blum, Linda M. *Between Feminism and Labor: The Significance of the Comparable Worth Movement.* Berkeley: University of California Press, 1991.

Brownmiller, Susan. *Against Our Will: Men, Women, and Rape.* New York: Bantam Books, 1976.

Burstyn, Varda, ed. *Women Against Censorship.* Toronto: Douglas & McIntyre, 1985.

Chappell, Duncan, ed. *Forcible Rape: The Crime, the Victim, and the Offender.* New York: Columbia University Press, 1977.

Cleaver, Eldridge. *Soul on Ice.* New York: McGraw-Hill, 1967.

Costa, Dallas. *The Power of Women and the Subversion in the Community.* Bristol: Falling Wall Press, 1972.

Cox, Nicole and Silvia Federici. *Counter-Planning from the Kitchen: Wages for Housework*. Bristol: Falling Wall Press.

Crean, Susan, ed. *Twist and Shout: A Decade of Feminist Writings in This Magazine*. Toronto: Second Story Press, 1992.

Dean, Charles W., Mary de Bruyn-Kops, and Charles C. Thomas, eds. *The Crime and Consequences of Rape*. Springfield, Ill.: Thomas, 1982.

Deane, H. A. *Justice: Compensatory and Distributive*. New York: Columbia University Press, 1974.

d'Souza, Dinesh. *Illiberal Education: The Politics of Race and Sex on Campus*. New York: Free Press, 1991.

Dworkin, Andrea. *Our Blood: Prophecies and Discourses on Sexual Politics*. New York: Harper & Row, 1976.

____. *Pornography: Men Possessing Women*. 2d ed. New York: Plume Book, 1989.

Dye, Thomas. *Understanding Public Policy*. 2d ed. Englewood Cliffs, N.J.: Prentice Hall, 1975.

Epstein, Richard. *Forbidden Ground: The Case Against Employment Discrimination Laws*. Cambridge, Mass.: Harvard University Press, 1992.

Engels, Friedrich. *The Origins of Family, Private Property, and the State*. Moscow: Progress, 1948.

Evans, Sara M. and Barbara J. Nelson, eds. *Wage Justice: Comparable Worth and the Paradox of Technocratic Reform*. Chicago: University of Chicago Press, 1989.

Faludi, Susan. *Backlash: The Undeclared War Against American Women*. New York: Crown, 1991.

Firestone, Shulamith. *The Dialectic of Sex: The Case for Feminist Revolution*. New York: Morrow, 1970.

Florman, Samuel C. *Blaming Technology: The Irrational Search for Scapegoats*. New York: St. Martin's Press, 1981.

Friedan, Betty. *The Feminine Mystique*. New York: Norton, 1963.

____. *The Second Stage*. New York: Summit Books, 1981.

Goldman, Emma. *Anarchism and Other Essays*. New York: Dover, 1969.

Gordon, Linda. *Heroes of Their Own Lives: The Politics and History of Family Violence*. New York: Viking, 1988.

Gordon, Margaret T. and Stephanie Riger. *The Female Fear*. New York: Free Press, 1989.

Graham, Hugh Davis. *Civil Rights and the Presidency: Race and Gender in American Politics, 1960–1972*. New York: Oxford University Press, 1992.

Grauerholz, Elizabeth and Mary A. Koralewski, eds. *Sexual Coercion: A Sourcebook on Its Nature, Causes, and Prevention*. Lexington, Mass.: Lexington, 1991.

Greer, Germaine. *The Female Eunuch*. London: MacGibbon & Kee, 1970.

Griffin, Susan. *Rape: The Power of Consciousness*. New York: Harper and Row, 1979.

Gross, Barry R., ed. *Reverse Discrimination*. Buffalo: Prometheus, 1977.

Groth, A. Nicholas and Jean H. Birnbaum. *Men Who Rape: The Psychology of the Offender*. New York: Plenum Press, 1979.

Hansen, Karen V. and Ilene J. Philipson, eds. *Women, Class, and the Feminist Imagination: A Socialist-Feminist Reader*. Philadelphia: Temple University Press, 1990.

Hewlett, Sylvia Ann. *A Lesser Life: The Myth of Women's Liberation in America*. New York: William Morrow, 1986.

Hursch, Carolyn J. *The Trouble with Rape*. Chicago: Nelson-Hall, 1977.

Hutner, Frances C. *Equal Pay for Comparable Worth: The Working Woman's Issue of the Eighties*. New York: Praeger, 1986.

Hynes, Patricia, ed. *Reconstructing Babylon: Essays on Women and Technology*. Bloomington: Indiana University Press, 1991.

Iannone, A. Pablo, ed. *Contemporary Moral Controversies in Business*. New York: Oxford University Press, 1989.

Jacobus, Mary, Evelyn Fox Keller, and Sally Shuttleworth, eds. *Body/Politics: Women and the Discourses of Science*. New York: Routledge, 1990.

Johnston, Jill. *Lesbian Nation: The Feminist Solution*. New York: Simon & Schuster, 1973.

Kammer, Jack. *Good Will Toward Men*. New York: St. Martin's Press, 1994.

Kaufman, Sue. *Diary of a Mad Housewife*. New York: Random House, 1967.

Kelly, Liz. *Surviving Sexual Violence*. Minneapolis: University of Minnesota Press, 1988.

Leidholdt, Dorchen and Janice G. Raymond, eds. *Sexual Liberals and the Attack on Feminism*. New York: Pergamon Press, 1990.

Livernash, E. Robert, ed. *Comparable Worth: Issues and Alternatives*. Washington, D.C.: Equal Employment Advisory Council, 1980.

Lovelace, Linda. *Out of Bondage*. Secaucus, N.J.: Stuart, 1986.

Lystad, Mary, ed. *Violence in the Home: Interdisciplinary Perspectives*. New York: Brunner/Mazel, 1986.

MacKinnon, Catharine A. *Feminism Unmodified: Discourses on Life and Law*. Cambridge, Mass.: Harvard University Press, 1987.

_____. *Only Words*. Cambridge, Mass.: Harvard University Press, 1993.

_____. *Toward a Feminist Theory of the State*. Cambridge, Mass.: Harvard University Press, 1989.

Maguire, Daniel C. *A New American Justice: Ending the White Male Monopolies*. Garden City, N.Y.: Doubleday, 1980.

Manhart, Mary Ann, ed. *Rape: The First Sourcebook for Feminists*. Report from the Workshop on Self-Defense.

Martin, Del. *Battered Wives*. Rev. ed. Volcano, Calif.: Volcano Press, 1981.

Marx, Karl. *Capital*. Middlesex: Penguin, 1976.

McElroy, Wendy, ed. *Freedom, Feminism, and the State: An Overview of Individualist Feminism*. Rev. ed. New York: Holmes & Meier, 1991.

_____. *XXX: A Woman's Right to Pornography*. New York: St. Martin's Press, 1995.

McLeod, Eileen. *Women Working: Prostitution Now*. London: Croom Helm, 1982.

Millett, Kate. *Sexual Politics*. Garden City, N.Y.: Doubleday, 1970.

Milunsky, Aubrey, ed. *Genetics and the Law, II: National Symposium on Genetics and the Law*. New York: Plenum Press, 1980.

Morgan, Robin, ed. *Sisterhood Is Powerful: An Anthology of Writings from the Women's Liberation Movement*. New York: Random House, 1970.

Okin, Susan Moller. *Justice, Gender, and the Family*. New York: Basic Books, 1989.

O'Neill, William L. *Everyone Was Brave: A History of Feminism in America*. New York: Quadrangle, 1974.

Paglia, Camille. *Sex, Art, and American Culture*. New York: Vintage Books, 1992.

_____. *Sexual Personae: Art and Decadence from Nefertiti to Emily Dickinson*. New York: Vintage Books, 1991.

Parrot, Andrea and Laurie Bechhofer, eds. *Acquaintance Rape: The Hidden Crime*. New York: John Wiley, 1991.

Pateman, Carole. *The Sexual Contract*. Stanford: Stanford University Press, 1988.

Peck, Ellen. *The Baby Trap*. New York: D. Geis Assoc., 1971.

Perutz, Kathrin. *Marriage Is Hell*. New York: Morrow, 1972.

Pheterson, Gail, ed. *A Vindication of the Rights of Whores*. Seattle: Seal Press, 1989.

Price, Lisa S. *In Women's Interest: Feminist Action and Institutional Change*. Vancouver: Women's Research Center, 1988.

Ratcliff, Kathryn Strother, ed. *Healing Technology: Feminist Perspectives*. Ann Arbor: University of Michigan Press, 1989.

Rawls, John. *A Theory of Justice*. Cambridge: Harvard University Press, 1971.

Raymond, Janice G. *Women as Wombs: Reproductive Technologies and the Battle Over Women's Freedom*. San Francisco: Harper, 1993.

Rich, Adrienne. *Of Woman Born: Motherhood as Experience and Institution*. London: Virago, 1977.

Roback, Jennifer. *A Matter of Choice: A Critique of Comparable Worth by a Skeptical Feminist*. New York: Priority Press, 1986.

Schultz, Leroy G. and Charles C. Thomas, eds. *Rape Victimology*. Springfield, Ill: Thomas, 1975.

Sears, Hal D. *The Sex Radicals: Free Love in High Victorian America*. Lawrence, Kansas: Regents Press, 1977.

Sexual Harassment: *A Report on the Sexual Harassment of Students*. Washington, D.C.: Report of the National Advisory Council of Women's Educational Programs, 1980.

Sheehy, Gail. *Hustling: Prostitution in Our Wide Open Society*. New York: Delacorte Press, 1973.

Sherman, Howard. *Radical Political Economy: Capitalism and Socialism from a Marxist-Humanist Perspective*. New York: Basic Books, 1972.

Soble, A., ed. *The Philosophy of Sex: Contemporary Readings*. Totowa, N.J.: Rowman and Littlefield, 1980.

Sommers, Christina Hoff. *Who Stole Feminism?: How Women Have Betrayed Women*. New York: Simon & Schuster, 1994.

_____. *Preferential Policies: An International Perspective*. New York: Morrow, 1990.

Spallone, Patricia and Deborah Lynn Steinberg, eds. *Made to Order: The Myth of Reproductive and Genetic Progress*. Oxford: Pergamon Press, 1987.

Steinem, Gloria. *Revolution from Within: A Book of Self-Esteem*. Boston: Little, Brown, 1992.

U.S. Merit Systems Protection Board. *Sexual Harassment in the Federal Workplace: Is It a Problem?* Washington, D.C.: U.S. Government Printing Office, 1981.

U.S. Merit Systems Protection Board. *Sexual Harassment in the Federal Government: An Update*. Washington, D.C.: U.S. Government Printing Office, 1988.

Wall, Edmund, ed. *Sexual Harassment: Confrontations and Decisions*. Buffalo: Prometheus Books, 1992.

Whiteford, Linda M. and Marilyn L. Poland, eds. *New Approaches to Human Reproduction: Social and Ethical Dimensions*. Boulder: Westview Press, 1989.

Index